The Strange Secret of the Big Time

Frosty Westering

Big Five Productions

Tacoma, Washington

The Strange Secret of the Big Time
published by Big Five Productions

© 2005 by Frosty Westering
ISBN: 0-9708257-3-0

Cover art/photo by www.AlaskaStock.com
Interior graphics design by Terry Marks Design

Unless otherwise indicated, scripture quotations are from: New International Version 1984 by International Bible Society

Printed in the United States of America

For information contact:
Big Five Productions
P.O. Box 45553
Tacoma, WA 98444
Website: http://coachfrosty.com

First printing 2005

05 06 07 08 09 10—7 6 5 4 3 2 1 0

To my loving wife Donna
and Our Family who have always helped
Make The Big Time Where We Are

ATTAWAY Cheers for Our All Star Team

These ATTAWAY cheers are for special people who made outstanding contributions in making this book a reality. They shared their belief in Making The Big Time Where They Are by driving the Blue Car on the Success Road each day of their lives. Their enthusiasm and excitement for life is a refreshing witness revealed through their positive lifestyle. Their contributions have truly been a "want to" all the way—a genuine labor of love.

Over the years I've saluted scores of coaches, players and people with Attaways and now it is my privilege to salute this special team of people with our classic cheer.

HEY STRANGE SECRET TEAM—
GO STRANGE SECRET TEAM
ATTAWAY! — ATTAWAY!

★ **Donna Westering** — My loyal and loving wife whose continued support and encouragement has kept me on track during the entire process of the book.
I love you Donna—ATTAWAY

★ **Sue Westering**— My dynamic daughter whose love and belief along with her special talents is what made this book what it is. Her second effort made everything fit together.

I love you Sue—ATTAWAY

★ **Brad Westering**— My talented son whose continued support and insights have made the writing of this book a joy.

I love you Brad—ATTAWAY

★ **Layne Nordgren**— My good friend and outstanding, creative computer expert. He was a clutch player and key performer in the entire process of the book.

Way to go Layne—ATTAWAY

★ **Terry Marks**— A former collegiate football player of mine with a special graphic design talent. He lives the belief of this book and his graphic work is Big Time.

ATTAWAY Terry

★ **Eric Weber**— Once again as with the first book, Eric gave excellent professional assistance and expertise in making this book Big Time.

ATTAWAY Eric

★ **Jim and Holly Johnson— Scott and Susan Westering—Gary and Stacey Spani—Chad and Michelle Johnson (are all on our family team)**—Their love and encouraging support was KEY as they live their lives Making The Big Time Where They Are. They all read various versions of the book and gave valuable insights and feedback that was incorporated in the final draft.

I love you XXL—ATTAWAY Family

★ **Heather Linderman—** My terrific granddaughter whose patience, writing talent and computer skills assisted me with the early versions of the book.

I love you Heather—ATTAWAY

★ **Jennifer Barrow—** Her excellent editing and conversation writing expertise has made the book easy to read and understand.

ATTAWAY—Jennifer

★ **JoAnne Davis—** Her work on the early stages of the book in putting stories, poems and other materials into book form was a big contribution.

ATTAWAY— JoAnne

★ **Angie Zurcher and the PLU Bookstore Team**— Their continued support in making this book happen was very much appreciated.
ATTAWAY— *Angie and Team*

★ **Steve Ridgway, Larry Green, Doug Burton, Doug Grant, Mark Mininger, Steve Thomas, Nick Dawson and Lauralee Hagen**— Eight very "special people" who continue to make the Big Time in their lives through their faith and sharing lifestyles.
ATTAWAY

★ **The hundreds of players and coaches whom I've been associated with over the years**— Your inspiration and perspiration made our years together Big Time.
ATTAWAY—ATTAWAY

A Note from BIG 5 Productions

Since Frosty wrote MAKE THE BIG TIME WHERE YOU ARE, we have been asked on many occasions when there would be a follow-up book. He shared in his first book the powerful idea and life-changing concepts on how a person can enjoy and succeed in their life more fully by learning how to travel on what Frosty refers to as the "Success Road of Life" and not the "Road to Success" which seemingly is all around us. We believe there is a big difference. We have learned over the years that simplicity and meaningful repetition are keys to understanding and bringing about change. This new book not only accomplishes that but expands these ideas and concepts in new ways.

Once again, the key idea of the BIG TIME is that--*it is not a place; it is the state of our heart.* It is our innermost thoughts, feelings, and beliefs that define who we really are. We can make our lives BIG TIME regardless of our situations once we believe it and learn how to do it.

Like a car, we can all use fine-tuning. Its engine needs regular check-ups and maintenance if it is to continue to perform at a high-level. Our hope is that this book will be a fine-tuning for you giving you specific adjustments that can make all the difference. Possibly it will be a complete overhaul to your perspective on life, work, relationships, and success. Whatever is the case, may you run more smoothly, more efficiently, and with added power as these truths sink deeper into your heart and are revealed through your life.

Contents

The New Challenge

The French playwright Victor Hugo once stated,

There is nothing more powerful than— an idea whose time has come.

The right idea at the right time can change your life in a way only *real change* occurs—from the inside out. That is what I believe this book can help you do.

The key idea of my first book was that you *Make the Big Time Where You Are* by realizing that the big time is not a place, but the state of your heart. Once you understand and believe this, you will change your attitude toward life. This is then reflected through your thoughts, feelings, and lifestyle choices but you must choose to live it, not just talk about it. There's a saying – "You can lead a horse to water, but you can't make him drink." However there's another line to that saying – "But you sure can make him thirsty." I believe this book will make you thirsty enough to live the BIG TIME IDEA and find the genuine HEART POWER that you really have inside of you.

When we listen and respond to the unselfish desires of our heart, we start to experience new joy and fulfillment as never before. We now become *go-givers* rather than just *go-getters*. We discover that the true joy of having is in sharing regardless of how much or how little it may be. This is the deepest sense of satisfaction and fulfillment we can have in life. It's God's math—the more we divide, the more we multiply.

These precious heartbeat values, however, can easily get drowned out by the loud, heavy, self-oriented drumbeat of society. It will constantly push us to march to the beat of "it's all about me," and without realizing it, we are being led into a no-win mind-set and a continually restless lifestyle.

My prayer is that this book will help you learn to march to the beat of a different drummer—one that will inspire you to use your own unique God-given talents in new ways.

This new adventure we will take together will also help you understand...*The Strange Secret of the Big Time* that can change your life forever.

Believe me, it's a WINNER!

Frosty

Chapter 1

The New Adventure Begins...

It was mid-morning as the United Boeing 757 passed over the Cascade Mountain Range in the clear summer sky. It was beginning its descent in preparation for landing at Sea-Tac Airport.

Sitting by the window near the front of the plane, Gary and Dan looked out and saw snowcapped Mt. Rainier in its entire splendor. It appeared so close that they felt like they could stand right on top of it. Looking further down the range, they could see three other majestic mountains in the distance. It was truly a spectacular sight.

Both Gary and Dan were looking forward to the upcoming weekend with Frosty, who would be meeting them at the airport. Several years before, Gary had experienced an inspiring breakaway weekend in the mountains with Frosty that had changed his outlook and attitude on life. He had learned, believed, and applied the powerful ideas, positive thought patterns, and dynamic actions Frosty had shared with him.

Since that time he and his family had moved to the Midwest, where they were experiencing a joy and fulfillment in their lives that they never had before. Gary's business was thriving, and his relationships with his family, staff, and friends as well as other facets of his life were going well.

Gary had met Dan during the past year on the golf course where they played regularly each week, and they had become friends.

Dan was a tall, outgoing man with a seemingly pleasing personality; however, he was highly competitive and would lose his temper quite easily when things weren't going well. He continually put others down and would shift any blame away from himself, alienating him from his business associates as well as his family.

As Gary got to know Dan better, he had started to share some of Frosty's key ideas that had made such a difference in his life—concepts like the Models of Winning, Success Road, The Potential Performance Gap, and Making the Big Time Where You Are. Dan had listened, but didn't really understand the concepts, and while they sounded interesting, he didn't really believe you could think or act like this and be successful in the highly competitive dog-eat-dog world.

One afternoon after playing eighteen holes of golf, Gary and Dan were sitting by themselves in the clubhouse. Dan started opening up and sharing many personal struggles, stressful situations, anger, and disappointments in his life. His business was faltering. He had lost several good staff associates as well as some good friends through heated discussions, confrontations, and differences of opinion. His relationships with his wife and two children were also severely strained. He felt he was in too many no-win situations and was losing the competitive drive that had gotten him on his road to success. Life was simply not good.

After listening for some time, Gary asked Dan an important question. Would he consider flying out to the Northwest, meeting Frosty, and being a part of a breakaway weekend like he had experienced some years before?

Dan listened, but was skeptical and felt very defensive. He didn't want to make himself vulnerable and share many of his inner beliefs and feelings to someone he had never met. Gary shared the inspiring, positive, life-changing experience he'd had with his good friend Frosty in the Cascade Mountains some years ago. He was so convincing that the next morning Dan called and told Gary that he would like to go. Gary was excited—he called Frosty and arranged this upcoming weekend.

The United plane landed at Sea-Tac Airport and taxied to the terminal. Dan suddenly felt very indecisive. He wasn't sure he really wanted to do this, for he would be exposing his many weaknesses and inadequacies, which he had never done before.

As Gary and Dan came out of the jetway and onto the concourse, Frosty and his good friend Cliff were there to meet them. Both were wearing eye-catching brown and white shell leis around their necks, and the first thing they did as they greeted Gary and Dan was to place the same kind of leis around their necks and give them a big hug like a Hawaiian Aloha greeting. This was a surprising and friendly gesture, and they both felt the warm welcome.

After picking up the luggage, everyone got into the blue Chevrolet van and were on their way.

Frosty started the conversation.

"I wanted you both to meet Cliff today. He's a good friend of mine and a special kind of man. Cliff is an elite athlete and one of the top martial art black belts in the world. More than that, though, he is the owner, director, and master of his own academy. He teaches hundreds of people, young and old, each year how to live a more enjoyable, fulfilling, and productive life."

Cliff joined in. "Frosty and I have a unifying belief that makes our relationship special. It's from Scripture, Proverbs 27:17, 'As iron sharpens iron, so we sharpen each other.' We respect, share, enjoy, and learn so much from one another.

"It will be a real pleasure for me to be with you and share part of your breakaway experience. I'll come down tomorrow to the beach cottage where you'll be staying."

Gary's eyes lit up. "So we're going to the ocean this time instead of the mountains?"

"Yes," Frosty said. "Our family has a special place at the ocean that is right on the beach. Well, let's say it's right *above* the beach, and the sundeck faces west. We have a great view of the sunsets and afterglows, and there is a surprise view a short way down the beach."

"What is it?" Gary asked.

"Let's just wait and see." Frosty smiled. "Cliff can't be with us until tomorrow afternoon, but I wanted you to meet him and have him share with us a classic story to start off our adventure."

Gary looked at Dan, and they both smiled. Gary had told Dan they would hear some great stories, poems, and illustrations that would make key ideas, principles, and concepts come to life.

We pulled off at the next exit, drove a short distance, and stopped at a small park with large shade trees and several picnic tables.

We all got out and sat down on one side of a picnic table. Cliff had taken a small cooler from the van and placed it on the other side of the table facing Gary and Dan. He took out two teacups with lids on them and a teapot. He placed them on top of the cooler and took the lids off the cups. He then looked Dan and Gary in the eye and began to tell his story...

Chapter 2

The Empty Cup...

A business executive was always trying to gain the edge over his competitors in any way he could. He had heard that a certain wise Grand Master had the key to the COMPETITIVE EDGE in life, which he believed could be of immense value to him.

He flew over to Shanghai, China, where the Grand Master lived, and was able to set up a meeting with him at his home.

When he arrived, he was met at the door by one of the Master's servants, who directed him to take off his shoes and put on the slippers he gave him. He then led him into the living room, where the Grand Master was sitting with his legs crossed on a soft oriental rug. The Grand Master beckoned the executive to come in and sit on the rug facing him.

"I have come a long way to see you, Grand Master," he began, "for I have heard that you have the key to the COMPETITIVE EDGE in life. I know many of the tricks of my profession and different ways to compete for THE EDGE, but I am told you can give me the master key to them all."

At that moment the servant brought in a small lap table with a tray, a teapot, and two cups.

The Grand Master said, "We need to pour a cup of tea before we begin."

"I am a very busy man, Grand Master. I don't have time for tea. I just want to know the secret of the Competitive Edge."

Without saying anything, the Grand Master began pouring the tea into one of the cups, and it immediately started overflowing on the tray. [Cliff was doing the same thing, pouring tea into one of the cups on the cooler, which was also overflowing onto the picnic table.]

Dan, watching and listening intently, exclaimed, "The cup is running over! It's running over—no more will go in!"

Cliff nodded and stopped pouring.

The Grand Master stopped pouring when the executive had called out the same words. He then held up the second cup, which was empty [Cliff did the same.]

The Grand Master then looked into the eyes of his guest [Cliff looked into Dan's eyes] and calmly said, "Like this cup, your mind is full of so many things. Until you empty your cup, like this second one, no more can go in. Likewise, until you empty your mind—

YOU CANNOT RECEIVE ANYTHING

The Parable of the Empty Cup

Dan had been completely immersed in the story. He realized that it was really about him. Cliff had so clearly illustrated the meaning of the empty cup. Dan now realized that he had had a full cup most of his life. If he was ever going to change for the better, he was going to have to empty his cup. This meant having an open mind and not being afraid to change.

"I hope you got the message from Cliff's story of the empty cup," Frosty said, "for we are going to share with you four valuable BLUEPRINTS for LIFE with the tools and materials to build them. You will then be surprised when a STRANGE SECRET is revealed to you, and when it is—

YOU WILL NEVER BE THE SAME

Dan and Gary looked at each other wide-eyed.

Everyone got back in the van and drove for about a half hour into the city, stopping at Cliff's marshal arts academy. Cliff bid the guys good-bye and reiterated that he would join them tomorrow afternoon.

Frosty, Gary, and Dan then drove west from the city for about an hour, turning off the main highway onto a scenic ocean drive. They followed the shoreline for several miles and soon pulled off to an ocean cottage right above the beach.

Frosty tossed the cottage keys to Gary and said he was going down to the nearby country store and would be back in a short time to help unload the van and get settled.

As Frosty left, Gary and Dan opened the side door to the cottage. As they stepped inside, they saw that they were in a large, comfortable family room with a wood beam ceiling. A large rock fireplace filled the far wall. A long sofa and two easy chairs were circled around it on a large, colorful braided rug. They looked to the left where they saw two long glass sliding doors that led out to a spacious sundeck over the beach.

On the other half of that wall was a knotty pine kitchen with cupboards that had copper pans hanging from them and two big windows on the ocean side. The kitchen was separated from the rest of the room by an eight-foot-long island counter with stools in front of it.

Gary and Dan walked to the sliding doors, unlocked them, and stepped out onto the sundeck. A large, bright multicolored patio umbrella with a table and chairs beneath it was in the center of the deck, and a double barbecue grill sat off to the side. The deck was enclosed with a white waist-high wooden rail.

"What an awesome view!" Gary exclaimed. They were about thirty feet above the white sand beach. They looked to their left and about a quarter-mile down could see a high monolith rock as high and as wide as a football field with hundreds of seagulls perched on and flying around it. Encircling the big rock were other rocks up to twenty feet high. The tide was going out, and the beach was over eighty yards wide. Looking the other direction, the beach went for about a half a mile and circled out around several high cliffs.

As they were enjoying the view, Frosty returned and joined them on the deck.

"Well, what do you think?"

Gary replied, "Frosty, it's a breathtaking view."

"Wait until you see the sunset. The forecast is for clear skies and a few scattered clouds for the next several days. The sunsets and afterglows are sensational, and maybe, just maybe, we'll see the green flash."

"What's the green flash?" Dan asked.

"Well, it's a rare atmospheric phenomenon that occurs at sunset—it doesn't happen very often. When conditions are right and there is a clear sky on the horizon, a few seconds before the top edge of the setting sun disappears from view, a brilliant emerald green color appears. It doesn't last very long, about three or four seconds, but believe me, it's spectacular.

"Let's get our gear out of the van, put on shorts and T-shirts, and go to the beach," Frosty said.

At the other end of the cottage were three bedrooms with double bunk beds and a bathroom. They put their gear in them, changed, and then walked down the twenty wooden steps beside the cottage to the beach. Frosty gave both Gary and Dan a tan leather pouch.

"I'd like us to beach comb and pick up some rocks of different color and shapes and put them in these pouches."

They walked down the beach toward the huge rock and felt exhilarated by the cool ocean breeze. As they reached it, they waded out in knee-deep water to the lower rock formations, where they found many colorful and unique-shaped rocks to put in their pouches.

Mid-afternoon they returned to the cottage for a great sub sandwich lunch with chips and sodas out on the sundeck under the large umbrella. It was truly a relaxing time. Dan and Gary were impressed, not just with the setting, but with the relaxed, comfortable atmosphere they were experiencing.

Chapter 3

Jump in the Wheelbarrow?

Gary explained, "Frosty, it's special for us be here with you this weekend. Dan and I have been looking forward to this and we're off to a great start."

Dan nodded his head and then shared the apprehensions and fears he'd had about coming. He was now excited to be a part of this time together and was eagerly looking forward to what was ahead.

Frosty handed each of them a blue loose-leaf notebook with their names on the side panel and a picture of a beautiful sunset on the front cover. It had dividers, one for the Right Stuff and the others for the 4 Blueprints for life, blank pages for notes, and a pencil pouch with colored pens and pencils.

"This will be your playbook for our breakaway weekend together, and Cliff and I will be your coaches. Take whatever notes you desire, and we'll have some Right Stuff to include with them. In fact, look at the first page and you'll see a sixteen-square grid. It will take on a different dimension to you as we look at it from time to time."

"Okay, Gary, where do we want to start?" Frosty asked.

"I've shared with Dan your Big Time idea and some of the key principles."

Dan joined in. "Since Cliff shared the empty cup story, I realized that I've had a full cup most of my life. I really didn't try to understand much of what Gary has shared in the past."

"That's okay, Dan. We've all had full cups at various times in our lives. The key is that you now realize it and are more open to learning. That's what the empty cup is all about. You must learn to keep an open mind, not be afraid to change, and yet not change just for the sake of change. Many older ideas and concepts are still some of the best because they have stood the test of time.

"You see there are actually five levels of learning.

Level one is MEMORY—we memorize something and we know it, but there's no real action, just information.

Level two is UNDERSTANDING—we know it and now have a basic understanding, but there is still no real action.

Level three is APPLICATION—we know it, understand it, and now know how to apply it, but still nothing happens until we reach level four.

Level four is BELIEF—when we really believe what we know, understand and can apply, then we take it to level five.

Level five is giving it our BEST SHOT—our best shot is making the best effort to be or do our best to apply what we've learned. However, our best shot sometimes isn't very good…but when we hang in there and keep at it, our best shot gets better and better. Level five learning really tells us who we are. It is our—

BELIEFS, VALUES, AND LIFESTYLE

Both Don and Gary jotted down their first notes on the five levels of learning, and I gave them a handout.

Five Levels of Learning

1. Memory
2. Understanding
3. Application
4. Belief
5. Your BEST SHOT

Let me tell you a fascinating story about belief...

A young sports promoter named Nick was traveling in Europe to find new talent for his outdoor entertainment company.

As he drove through a small city in France, he noticed a large crowd gathering in the downtown area. As he came closer he noticed that they were all looking up toward the sky. Looking up, Nick saw a man walking on a high-wire between two buildings some three hundred feet above. The man would walk forward and backward and then jump and land on the wire several times with the greatest of ease.

This man was truly an outstanding performer. When he had finished his performance, Nick introduced himself to the high-wire performer named Jacob. Nick explained to him that he owned an outdoor entertainment company and had a great idea that would attract thousands of people and that he would be able to pay Jacob a large fee for his performance.

The plan was to string a high-wire across the American side of Niagara Falls, which was one thousand feet from one side to the other. He would then have Jacob walk across and back over the falls, more than two hundred feet above the jagged rocks below. It would be a death-defying act. Jacob thought for a few moments—

He was confident and believed in his balancing ability. And this would be a great opportunity to perform his talents in front of thousands of people, so he agreed to do it.

After several months of publicizing the event, the day came. Thousands of people were in attendance. After some preliminary events, Nick announced to the large crowd over the loudspeaker what Jacob would attempt to do. Jacob then amazed the crowd with his unbelievable high-wire walk, going completely across and back over the falls and the jagged rocks below.

As Jacob came to the end of the wire and onto the landing, Nick was ecstatic.

"Despite the doubts of many of the people I've talked to, I was sure you could walk over the falls on the high-wire."

Jacob replied, "I really believed I could do it. In fact, I believe I can cross the wire with this wheelbarrow I have with me on the landing."

Nick smiled and said, "Do you really believe you can do that?"

"Yes, Nick, I can do it with this wheelbarrow. Do you believe I can?"

Nick looked at the wheelbarrow and slowly nodded his head.

Jacob asked him again, "Do you really believe I can do it?"

Nick nodded again and said, "I believe you can do it."

Jacob paused for several seconds, looked Nick in the eye, and said, "Okay, then…

JUMP IN THE WHEELBARROW!

"That's just what you have to do," Frosty said. **"BELIEVE—REALLY BELIEVE!** But you have to know *what* or *whom* you believe in, for this means putting your trust in someone or something.

While we are imperfect people, we can earn trust through love and caring, honesty and sincerity, dependability and respectfulness. There is no trust without US. Trust is the most valuable relationship quality you can acquire from someone."

Frosty had a blue sports bag by his chair, and he reached down and pulled out a miniature wheelbarrow and set it in the middle of the table.

"It would take real courage to jump in and ride in the wheelbarrow with Jacob on the high-wire, for you are putting your complete trust in another person."

Dan added to his notes,

WHOM DO I TRUST?

Frosty continued, "Today there are so many lifestyles, values, and pseudo-beliefs that are being advocated and promoted today by all kinds of different people and organizations. They're all trying to get your attention and allegiance by extolling their virtues. Many are self-centered—the so-called "it's all about me" lifestyle. They can be very persuasive—some are seductively subtle—but if you buy into their rhetoric, you will soon feel deceived and find yourself caught in a no-win life spiral at a very young age."

Frosty continued, "Relationships are the key to your beliefs and to a fulfilling lifestyle. It's sad that many people really don't have any. It's been shown that sixty percent of our relationships with people are at what's known as the *formal level*—friendly small talk, but no real connection and a closed sharing with others. Thirty percent are at the *informal level*. These are with job-related associates or friends in various social settings. Still, there's a closed sharing of ourselves with others at this level. Five percent of our relationships are at the *confidence level*. Here we have close friends that we have confidence in, and we begin to take the lid off our box and start to open up and share about ourselves, our beliefs and concerns, our family, and our life."

Dan and Gary were intent as Frosty laid out the facts. "Only five percent of our relationships are at the *trust level*. These relationships are based on honesty, respect, and friendship. At this level we are open and share about our beliefs, our values, and ourselves. The lid is off our box in a trust relationship—yet I'm sorry to say that many people never have *any* confidential or trust relationships in their lives.

"Let me share with you a story about trust...

There was a dad who had a loving trust relationship with his son over the years, and he wanted to show his son an important example about trust. The father told him to stand with his arms held out to his side, away from his body, to close his eyes, and then to fall back into the arms of his dad.

Without hesitation the young boy closed his eyes, lifted his arms, and fell back into the arms of his dad, who caught him before he hit the floor. The dad looked into his son's eyes and said, "That's what trust is all about—knowing that you can depend on someone who really loves and cares about you."

Another dad did the same thing—only he had little or no relationship with his son and what he did have was negative and antagonistic.

When his son fell back, the dad didn't catch him, and he hit the floor with a painful thud.

That dad then said, "See there, you learned a lesson. Don't trust anyone."

Gary and Dan shook their heads.

"This last example is a sad commentary on learning about trust. If key relationships can't be built on confidence and trust, life becomes very superficial. It's lonely and has no real meaning. Relationships are what life is really all about, and without any genuine ones, there is no joy and fulfillment."

"We all need mentors in our lives to help us develop trust. This usually starts with our mom or dad or other family members. However, there are other key people we respect and look up to that we should seek out and confide in. They can share wisdom and their perspective on life and can assist us with decision-making in the highs and lows of life.

"Other mentors can be of a different type. They are people we have never known personally, but by reading about them, seeing them on TV, or learning about them in other ways, we grow to admire and respect them for who they are, what they stand for, and what they do.

THEY ARE MODELS FOR US TO EMULATE

Frosty continued. "For many years, our college football team has been involved in a highly successful motivational mentoring program in elementary and middle schools in the lower socioeconomic area of Tacoma, Washington. A large percent of these young children are from one-parent or no-parent homes."

"Each year, over one hundred of our players and cheerleaders are involved. With the help of the teachers, we have developed a motivational inner game playbook for each grade level emphasizing positive attitudes, making right choices, teamwork, sportsmanship, citizenship, and self-discipline. The relationships between the young children and our players have become very special. Two times each season we bring the young students to our home games. To qualify to attend, they must complete all their goal-sets for that week and a second effort project. This is a *big deal* for the kids. After the game they get to visit our locker room, where our team gives them **ATTAWAY** cheers and **HIGH FIVES** for their accomplishments. Their eyes light up, and smiles are on their faces. Believe me—**IT IS BIG TIME!**

"Many times you never realize the real value of a program like this, but let me share with you one instance that has made it all worthwhile:

> It happened several years ago on one of our football trips to California. We were on a commercial flight, and I happened to be sitting next to a young businessman. He recognized me and started a conversation, telling me he had been in our mentoring program for three years and that it changed his life. The belief in himself that he gained through the program gave him the will to succeed. He was motivated to go on to community college and then graduated from a state university with a degree in business. He was now a computer analyst in the Silicon Valley and happily married with two kids.
>
> When we landed at LAX, I told our team to remain seated to let the other passengers get off the plane. I then called their attention to this young man and told them his story. We gave him a big ATTAWAY cheer as he went through a "Go Tunnel" while leaving the plane. It was great—even the flight crew cheered! He waited for us at the terminal, and when we had deplaned, we took pictures our him, our players, and our staff.
>
> It was a very special time.

After the story, Frosty gave Gary and Dan a handout on relationships to put in the Right Stuff section of their playbooks.

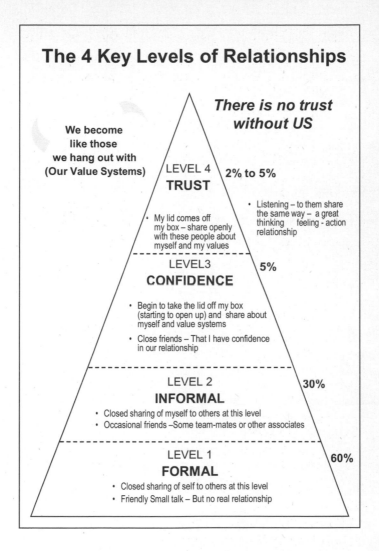

The 4 Key Levels of Relationships

There is no trust without US

We become
like those
we hang out with
(Our Value Systems)

LEVEL 4   2% to 5%
TRUST

- My lid comes off
  my box – share openly
  with these people about
  myself and my values

- Listening – to them share
  the same way – a great
  thinking   feeling - action
  relationship

LEVEL3   5%
CONFIDENCE

- Begin to take the lid off my box
  (starting to open up) and share about
  myself and value systems

- Close friends – That I have confidence
  in our relationship

LEVEL 2   30%
INFORMAL

- Closed sharing of myself to others at this level
- Occasional friends –Some team-mates or other associates

LEVEL 1   60%
FORMAL

- Closed sharing of self to others at this level
- Friendly Small talk – But no real relationship

Chapter 4

The Hidden Power... ?

Gary, Dan, and Frosty got up, stretched, and looked out at the impressive ocean view for a while. Eventually they settled back into our comfortable deck chairs, had a glass of iced tea, and resumed their conversation.

"Learning to communicate is one of the most important keys in developing relationships, and so many times what we think we are communicating is not really what is being understood at all," Frosty said. "Here is a humorous example that happened with our football team several years ago."

I'm always looking for various ways to make a key point, and using visual aids always enhances it. I wanted to show our team the dangers of alcohol to their body and the effects it would have on their personal fitness.

I asked Dr. Jerry Lerum, who was head of our biology department and also had had a son on our team, if he had any ideas. Jerry shared with me the "worm, water, and alcohol experiment." He guaranteed me it would be a great visual and that the results would be very clear.

At our next team meeting, I was all set to do the experiment. I had two large clear glasses on a table in the front of the room, one filled with water and the other with alcohol. I also had a small box with a large fish worm in it. I told our team what was in the glasses and to watch so they could see clearly what alcohol can do to your body.

I opened the small box and took out the six-inch fish worm and held it up in front of them. Then I dropped it in the water glass and held the glass up so everyone could see. The worm lazily moved around in the water. I then lifted the worm out of the water and put it in the glass of alcohol. I held the glass up for the team to clearly see, and in less than ten seconds, the worm was dead—rigor mortis set in quickly, and it stiffened as solid as a nail. My point, I thought, was very clear.

So I asked one of my offensive linemen in the front row, "What does this experiment show you?"

Without hesitating he said, "Coach Frosty, it looks to me like if you drink alcohol, **you won't have worms.**

The entire team, our staff, and I broke out in laughter.

Both Gary and Dan were laughing too.

"I hope I can communicate with you this weekend about our BIG TIME idea better than I did with the football team!"

"Frosty," Gary said, "let's talk about that power we need to discover in each of us. It's a power I didn't know I had until you shared it with me. As I learned to recognize and use this power in a positive way with all the other great things I learned during our last breakaway in the mountains, an exciting new adventure began in my life."

Dan looked puzzled and waited for me to respond.

"The power Gary is talking about is not recognized as a power. It is much like the man who didn't recognize the black rocks on his small farm as diamonds in their rough state. He sold his farm to search for diamonds at other places, never finding them, when there was actually an acre of diamonds all around him on the farm he once owned."

"We don't need to look other places for this power, for it is right here within us. And when we discover it, recognize it as a power, and use it in a positive way, it can change our lives in amazing ways. It is, however, disguised in ordinary ways and can be right in front of us, and yet we still don't see it. It can be demonstrated right before our very eyes, yet we do not see it with all its possibilities and wonder-working results. This power can change negatives into positives, depression into joy, and mediocrity into excellence."

The suspense was getting to Dan. "Tell me, Frosty, what is this power you're talking about?"

"Here it is, your own acre of diamonds. Dan, it's your **POWER OF CHOICE**! [1] Yes, choice is the greatest power God has given us, and

learning to use it in a strong and positive way will give our lives a new exciting dimension and direction."

"The majority of people don't recognize or use choice as a power in their lives. They let others or circumstances choose for them. They put themselves in many no-win situations. We live in a predominantly negative society and must learn who to believe and trust and what situations to get involved in."

CHOICE, NOT CHANCE
DETERMINES OUR DESTINY

"Let me tell you a story that relates to this."

A lone fisherman would go out on the lake in his small boat at daybreak one day each week. He would return in a relatively short time with a large number of fish, while the other fishermen on the lake seemed to catch very few. One morning, a game warden was at the lake and listened to the other fisherman talking about the lone fisherman who was getting all the fish.

The next week the game warden, disguised in old fishing gear, came to the lake at daylight and saw the lone fisherman getting into his small boat. He talked with him in a friendly manner and asked if he could go fishing with him. The lone fisherman looked around, didn't see anyone else, and told him he could come along.

They motored across the lake to the other side of a small island. The fisherman stopped the boat, lowered the anchor, opened his tackle box, and took out a small stick of dynamite. He lit it and tossed it in the water. The underwater explosion stunned all the fish near the boat, and they quickly rose to the surface.

The fisherman got out two nets and handed one to the game warden, who was sitting in the other end of the boat. "Here, get all the fish you want."

At that moment, the game warden's face became stern. He got out his badge and showed it to the fisherman. He told him he was breaking the most sacred fishing law and that anyone who did this would be fined one thousand dollars and would lose their fishing license for three years.

The fisherman looked at the game warden and said, "Is that right? Anyone who does this will get the same fine and lose their license?"

The game warden solemnly responded, "That's right, anyone. And I've caught you in the act."

The fisherman reached into his tackle box, took out another stick of dynamite, lit it, and tossed it into the game warden's lap.

"Well, are you going to sit there, or are you going to fish?"

Both Gary and Dan chuckled.

"You'd better know who you are with, where you are hanging out, and what you believe in so you don't get caught in these no-win situations. There are many people who will conform to almost anything. *They stand for a little and fall for a lot."*

Both Dan and Gary nodded their heads. They had put themselves in some of these situations before in their lives.

"You will have the opportunity to use your power of choice related to which situation you will involve yourself in."

Dan looked eager. "Frosty, I have emptied my cup and am ready to fill it with my power of choice."

"Okay, then—here we go!" Frosty said.

"You've heard about the two-minute drill in football. Well, we're going to do the one-minute drill. Turn back to the first page of your playbook, the one with the sixteen-square grid. Now, I'm telling you that there are more than sixteen squares—you have one minute to see how many you can find by restructuring them. When the one minute is up, write the number of squares you have found, and we'll talk about it later...

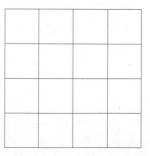

**HOW MANY SQUARES
CAN _YOU_ FIND IN A MINUTE?**

Chapter 5

The Magic Word...

Big Five

The hand diagram contains: CHALLENGE, CONFIDENCE, COMPARISON, ENTHUSIASM, CHOICE surrounding the center "Attitude is Everything"

Everything starts with what many have called the MAGIC WORD," Frosty said. "A word, when really understood and applied in a positive way, can change your life. Yes, that's what I said—CHANGE YOUR LIFE! I believe that this is the most important word in regard to the results we get in life."

"The magic word is *ATTITUDE*, and believe me, there are all kinds of attitudes out there. Many are negative, self-centered, and intimidating, so we'd better understand what our attitude really is. It is actually **the habit of the way we think. It affects how we feel and, in turn, the way we act.** It is the outer reflection of what's going on inside us. It is our mind's eye computer of our past experiences, which are stored in our subconscious mind. It is how we have responded and will respond to similar situations in the future. It is the mirror of our self-image.

"Let me show you a unique example of how important *ATTITUDE* is in our lives. Frosty handed them a page with the alphabet on it and a number assigned to each letter:

A-1, B-2, C-3, D-4, E-5, F-6, G-7, H-8, I-9, J-10, K-11, L-12, M-13, N-14, O-15, P-16, Q-17, R-18, S-19, T-20, U-21, V-22, W-23, X-24, Y-25, Z-26.

"Now take the word *ATTITUDE*. Give each letter its number equivalent, and then add them up."

A T T I T U D E

__ __ __ __ __ __ __ __ = __%

Both Gary and Dan did this. "That's an awesome illustration of the importance of attitude," Gary said.

Dan chimed in, "I didn't realize that attitude makes that big of a difference."

"It is our attitude more than anything else," Frosty said, "that determines our success or failure in any situation.

"Psychologists may disagree on various things, but there is one thing they all agree on: the importance of attitude. It is the key to achievement and success.

WE BECOME
WHAT WE THINK ABOUT

"Not many people really understand the value and power of our thoughts and the effect they have on our subconscious mind. Our subconscious mind is our own personal **supercomputer**. Like a computer, it will only give us back what we put in.

"We can compare our subconscious to a piece of land. You can plant corn or wheat in one half and plant deadly nightshade, a poisonous plant, in the other half. Both will grow and produce their many by-products. The land doesn't care what is planted—healthy crops or deadly poison.

"It is the same with our subconscious mind. It doesn't care what we put in it. Positive, worthwhile thoughts or critical, self-limiting ones. It is so much easier to be negative than positive, for we are in a world that has bought into the idea that by blowing out others' candles, ours will shine brighter."

Dan looked thoughtful. "It seems like there are a lot of people blowing out one another's candles."

Frosty nodded. "Without realizing it, we can also let society program our computer for us—the anger, controversy, violence, sex, and self-indulgent behavior we see so much on TV, in newspapers, on videos, at the movies, on the Internet, in video games, in magazines, and in high-powered commercials. It seems like today's outrage must continue to escalate to remain outrageous. The media continues to glorify self-indulgence.

"It is a plain and simple fact that we are the sum total of our thoughts and values at this time in our life. And we need to understand that the actions, feelings, and moods we have determine, in many ways, the actions, feelings, and moods of others towards us. It is our attitude toward life that determines life's attitude toward us."

"I spoke one time to a business group and noticed the word **GIGO** on cards next to individual computers. I asked the CEO what it meant, and he told me that it's an acronym for **Garbage In Garbage Out** that was used to remind them not to put garbage in their computer."

Dan and Gary were listening intently as Frosty continued. "I looked at **GIGO** for a moment and realized that it's like a self-fulfilling prophecy. You talk about garbage and you get garbage, regardless of whether you want it or not. 'I have an idea how you could change that,' I said. The CEO responded, 'We have hundreds of cards like this printed.' I told him that he wouldn't have to change the card, but change the *meaning* of the card. The meaning I'm talking about wouldn't be garbage in garbage out, but **Good In Good Out.** 'As much as possible, you want to tell people what you want them to do, not what you don't want them to do. I have even a better one—**God In God Out.** The CEO replied, 'From garbage to God, huh?' I said, 'That's right, you give **GIGO** its meaning—it's your choice!'"

Gary spoke up and said, "Frosty, I remember when you took a cassette tape and put it on top of my head. I really didn't understand what that was about until you explained it to me.

Frosty pulled out two cassette tapes from his blue sports bag and gave them to Gary. "Go ahead and demonstrate this to Dan."

Gary placed one cassette on Dan's head and held the other in his hand. "For years we have looked at and listened to these tapes of past experiences in our life, which are stored in our mind, over and over again. The ironic thing is that we didn't choose many of these tapes. In fact, you didn't choose the tape that's on your head right now. Many times these tapes have been dictated by time, place, and other people who actually chose them for us. For example, we didn't choose the time in history when we grew up in, where we lived, or what social status we were born into. We didn't choose our physical characteristics, our name, or our genetic talent potential. We also didn't choose many of the attitudes we have. Many times, we actually let others do it for us."

Gary continued, "Some things we did choose and they were based on the information and value system we had at that time. Some of them were good—some were not. It would be exciting to go back into our mind's eye computer and edit or delete some of the experiences of the past and record a new tape like the one in my hand. However this is very difficult to do.

"The real 'pay value' on what we can do is to use our power of choice from now on to edit our tapes where we can and, more important, to select new ones to record on, like the blank tape I have in my hand."

Frosty looked pleased at Gary's grasp of this concept. "Gary, that was a great way to share the cassette tape illustration. We must continuously remember: **WE BECOME WHAT WE THINK ABOUT.** But we need to be sure that we're the ones doing the thinking. Did you know that sixty percent of people don't really think or they let others think for them? Twenty-five percent of people *think* they think, but really don't. And only 10–15 percent of people really think on their own. This last group of people program their subconscious computer to make positive things happen in their lives—**and they do.**"

Frosty looked at Dan. "Let's start to record a new tape in our mind's eye computer, starting with a powerful idea—an idea that I believe can change your life. Yes, Dan, that's what I said—*change your life*. That's a powerful statement, but this is a powerful idea, and Gary is living proof of this reality. This idea will help you look at relationships, fulfillment, and success in new ways for what they can really be in your life. This powerful idea is:

MAKE THE BIG TIME
WHERE YOU ARE!

"Dan, when you start to see that the BIG TIME is not a place, like so many people think, but really a *state of your heart,* you'll see what I mean. Many people never really know their heart. It is that dynamic spirit within us that generates genuine faith, hope, and love, as well as desires, goals, and the excitement of life. When people find their own acre of diamonds right where they are, they find that—

IT'S NOT SOMETHING YOU GET,
IT'S SOMEONE YOU BECOME!

Frosty handed them a copy of the Big Time idea.

Make The BIG TIME Where You Are!

IT'S NOT A PLACE → IT'S THE STATE OF YOUR HEART!

IT'S NOT SOMETHING OR SOMEWHERE YOU GET →
IT'S SOMEONE YOU BECOME
IT'S A LIFESTYLE

IT ALL STARTS WITH OUR ATTITUDE (100%) - OUR HABIT OF THOUGHT
THAT AFFECTS OUR FEELINGS & ACTIONS
WE BECOME WHAT WE THINK ABOUT

OUR MIND IS **THE POWER OF CHOICE** OUR BIGGEST MUSCLE!

CHOICE NOT CHANCE DETERMINES OUR DESTINY.

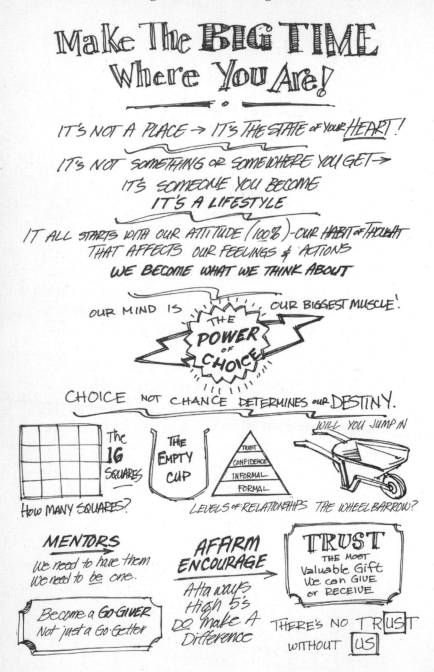

The **16** SQUARES
How MANY SQUARES?

THE EMPTY CUP

TRUST
CONFIDENCE
INFORMAL
FORMAL
LEVELS OF RELATIONSHIPS

WILL YOU JUMP IN
THE WHEELBARROW?

MENTORS
We need to have them.
We need to be one.

Become a Go-GIVER
Not just a Go-Getter

AFFIRM ENCOURAGE
Atta ways
High 5's
DO make A Difference

TRUST
THE MOST
Valuable Gift
We can GIVE
or RECEIVE

THERE'S NO TRUST
WITHOUT US

Chapter 6

Blueprint for Life #1: It's All About Winning

W e are going to learn how to **MAKE THE BIG TIME WHERE WE ARE** by playing the four attitude games of life," Frosty said. "Learning how to play these games in a new way will make a big difference in how you think, feel, and act, and believe me, the pay value will be big.

"Here are three action checks we've made out for each of you. Put your name and the date on the top lines, and at the end of our weekend or later on, when you are ready, endorse and cash them. You will start to immediately receive their ongoing value, which is priceless.

	Date: _____
Pay to the order of _____	fun
more joy and fulfullment	
WINNING ATTITUDE BANK	_____

	Date: _____
Pay to the order of _____	win
new levels of excellence	
WINNING ATTITUDE BANK	_____

	Date: _____
Pay to the order of _____	self image
new awareness of personal worth	
WINNING ATTITUDE BANK	_____

"All of us like to play games: sports games, video games, card games, board games, gambling games, and other games of all kinds. However, the games we are going to learn to play are the most important games of all. They are—

THE ATTITUDE GAMES OF LIFE

"And you know how important **attitude** is," Frosty said. "The first MAGIC WORD game is

BLUEPRINT FOR LIFE #1:
THE COMPARISON GAME

"This game is the basis of all the others and—

IT'S ALL ABOUT WINNING

Dan exclaimed, "I'm going to like this game!"

"Okay, let's get started. In football, the fundamentals of blocking, tackling, passing, receiving, and kicking are the keys to the development of any successful system of play. In any field of endeavor, specific fundamentals need to be performed at a high level. If not, the best systems in the world will not succeed. Learning to play this comparison game is *fundamental to all other life games.*"

Frosty moved the small wheelbarrow on the table to one side, reached into my blue bag, and brought our four bright red model cars and put them in a square in the middle of the table.

"The first model of winning we're going to talk about is the one that the majority of people know about and believe in. Since red is one of the most popular colors of cars, I chose it to represent this model. It's the classic mind-set that says:

WINNING ISN'T EVERYTHING; IT IS THE ONLY THING

Frosty picked up one of the red cars. "Drivers of this car believe that if they aren't the best, the champion, the first-place finisher, they're really no one. Second place, or any other place, has *no place* in their book. You are **number one or you are no one.** Several downtown billboards at the Olympic Games in Atlanta some years ago reflected this mind-set:

YOU DON'T WIN SILVER — YOU LOSE GOLD

"It was an in-your-face marketing technique that supposedly showed that elite athletes have the mind-set that if you aren't number one, you are a nobody. This totally contradicts the Olympic Creed of sportsmanship, respect, fair play, and the joy of the competitive experience. In other words, this arrogant way of thinking says that if you can't win, why compete? You may as well take your shoes and go home.

Frosty shook his head. "An interesting fact is that less than 6 percent of over eleven thousand

Olympic athletes receive gold. The other 14 percent who receive silver and bronze, along with the other 80 percent who are participants, would essentially be considered nobodies! These billboard signs were taken down during the competition at the request of the Olympic Committee.

"A mind-set of this type sees only the outcome as important. People have to prove themselves superior to feel secure and successful. When they, or who they support, aren't number one, they can easily become defensive and resentful.

"This red car travels on the ROAD TO SUCCESS. It's a highly visible road that is all around us. We are consistently being told that it will take us to the success place, wherever that might be. The road signs say that this is the way to go to win the success race."

Frosty looked at the guys, trying to determine if they were grasping the concept. "In sports, most teams, from the professionals to the Little Leagues, believe this is the way to go. It is the model of winning. It is also the predominant model in the business world, from big corporations to small entrepreneurs. In fact, it appears that anyone who is a competitor believes this is the only model of winning. It is what we see, hear, and read about all the time. In essence, it says that you have to endure the trip and follow this ROAD TO SUCCESS. This is the way to be number one, and if you don't follow this road, you will really be a no one."

Dan seemed confused. "Frosty, isn't that what competition is all about? Everyone wants to win in every game they play! Even if you're just playing computer games or checkers."

"Yes, Dan, that's true, however we really need to understand what winning and the competitive experience are all about."

Frosty lifted the small front hood of the red car in his hand to show the engine and continued. "This red car is powered by the highly competitive emphasis of comparing oneself to others and focusing on the final result—the belief that there is only one winner and that you only win when you defeat someone or anyone. It's very self-oriented and doesn't know any other way to win. You must compare and compete to show others how good you are. A key point to remember, however, is that we do not control someone or anyone.

"During the competitive experiences on this road to success, many frustrations, negative thought patterns, and emotions occur over and over again. These thought patterns influence life behavior and performance levels in various ways. Tension, stress, and anxiety are often present, and the fear of failure can have a constant negative effect on thoughts, feelings, and actions. This happens many times without a person even being aware of it. It is so much easier to fall into negative thought patterns (the put-down) than positive ones (the put-up). Red car people seem to think they are elevating themselves by putting others down—it makes them look good and others look bad. However, this is far from the truth, for the put-down demeans others and can alienate them. This puts red car people in many no-win situations."

Dan and Gary wrote in their playbooks review notes on the red car model of winning.

"Now let's make a major paradigm shift." Frosty reached into the sports bag and took out a bright blue model car and placed it on the table in the middle of the red cars. "The blue car represents another model of winning. As you know, there are far fewer blue cars then red ones. Just as there are a much smaller number of people who know, understand, and believe in this model of winning."

He picked up the blue car, "This car travels on a much different road then the red car and has a vastly different power source. This car travels on the

SUCCESS ROAD

The red car's ROAD TO SUCCESS is one where you have to reach the end of the road to experience any **pay value.**

"The blue car's SUCCESS ROAD is one on which you experience its **pay value** every day you travel it. The big difference is—

SUCCESS IS NOT AT THE END
OF THE ROAD; IT IS THE ROAD!

Dan wrinkled his brow in a questioning manner.

Frosty lifted the small hood on the blue car, "This car is powered by the excitement of personal achievement and the challenge of becoming one's BEST SELF, not by the red car's comparison to others. Achievement and excellence occur in the competitive arena, and *winning becomes a by-product.* It happens because of the trip the blue car travels on the SUCCESS ROAD. By focusing on competing with one's BEST SELF, exciting things start to happen in our lives, and the joy of the competitive experience increases. The key is that an individual is now in control of his point of effort, and his desires and goal-sets now become more meaningful and attainable."

Dan remarked, "This blue car is certainly a different model of winning that I didn't know about."

"That's true for most people, Dan," Frosty said. "They don't even know a blue car is in the race. Driving the blue car on the SUCCESS ROAD diminishes many of the pitfalls of the red car on its ROAD TO SUCCESS (tension, anxiety, fear, regret).

"In their place emerges a renewed confidence and well-being, as you travel on the SUCCESS ROAD. This is developed through encouragement, positive self-talk, and the building of strong affirmations. The desire to achieve steadily increases as one drives the blue car.

"Sure there are setbacks, disappointments, detours, flat tires, and engine repair with the blue car, however there is now *meaning* and *purpose*, which gives control over the direction and intensity of an individual's point of effort."

Frosty paused. "Believe me, this is BIG TIME."

He looked at both men, wondering if this concept was sinking in. "Another exciting by-product of the SUCCESS ROAD is the *Dynamic Double-Win,* which is bringing out the best in oneself and others. It increases confidence, raises morale, and brings excitement and positive feelings into the competitive arena. A key by-product is that it enhances performance levels and gives individuals a new awareness of personal worth in their lives."

Dan leaned forward. "I hear what you're saying, and it all sounds well and good, but we live in a red car world on the ROAD TO SUCCESS. Look at the model cars on the table. There are four red and one blue. That's the way it is, and that's the way people think and act. It's a jungle out there, and you've gotta look out for yourself.

IT'S SURVIVAL OF THE FITTEST

Frosty smiled. "You're right, this is the way many people think. However, life is more than surviving. It's enjoying and experiencing success in many new ways. You see, there is another car and another road in the SUCCESS RACE that most people don't even know about.

Well, it isn't that people don't know; it's that **they don't know they don't know!** If all we do is endure or tolerate the trip to the so-called destination in life, we really have missed the boat, or better yet, we're on the boat but are seasick most of the time."

Gary and Dan looked at each other.

"What I mean is this: The majority of people young and old struggle in far too many areas of their daily lives. They actually miss out on countless numbers of natural highs in ordinary things that are all around them because of their attitude toward life.

"What we're talking about is the way people think about winning. Many people don't know what it's like to feel like a winner because they really don't know what a winner is. I'm not talking about a winner in a sports contest or some business deal, but a winner when it really counts in the game of life. In fact there are many athletes, businesspeople, and others who win in their specific arena but do not know how to live a winning lifestyle in their own personal lives. As a result, they get all bent out of shape and struggle with many things in their lives that they don't need to.

"Once we learn that winning in everyday life is all about traveling on the SUCCESS ROAD, we can then make different choices that can change our lives in new and positive ways. As a result, to our surprise we have more fun, we perform at higher levels, and we feel better about ourselves because we are focusing our energy and talents on what we can control. These are the three checks I gave you."

Frosty pointed to their playbooks. "As in anything worthwhile in life, there is a price—no free lunches! The price for success is HARD WORK with a purpose.

"A large number of people with vague purpose in their lives do not want to pay this price. Their work ethic is 'good enough to get by is...good enough.' They accept a ho-hum quality of life and never experience the joys and benefits they could by paying the price of hard work.

"Here is an example of the "good enough to get by is good enough" mentality, only this time it wasn't even close to being good enough:

> It was finals week at a university just before Christmas. A young college guy who was taking the basic required classes didn't feel he needed to study much for the exams. He was doing okay in his classes, and okay for him was good enough.
>
> He went into one final exam and found that he didn't know much about the questions being asked. He guessed at many of the objective ones and had to leave many of the completion ones blank. As he finished the exam, he wrote a note to the professor on the last page.

Dear Professor Olsen,
Only God knows the answers to these questions—
Merry Christmas

Your student,
Jerry Wilson

He came back to school after the Christmas break and went to the departmental office to pick up his exam. When he picked it up, he noticed that there wasn't a grade on it, just a note from Professor Olsen telling him to look at the last page. He flipped the pages over and read,

Dear Jerry,
Thank you for your note—
God gets an A—you get an F

Happy New Year

Everyone laughed!

When the laughter had died down, Frosty began again. "There is a price that everyone needs to pay for excellence. If they don't, then they must accept lower levels of mediocrity and can easily fall into a negative lifestyle. Jerry didn't want to pay the price, and the result was obvious.

FAILING TO PREPARE IS PREPARING TO FAIL

"The joy of achievement, accomplishment, and excellence comes from working hard with a meaningful purpose. That means being dedicated to the job at hand and determined to give our BEST SHOT over and over again toward its successful completion.

"By taking satisfaction in working hard, we pay the price that brings out our BEST SELF. When we do this, it enhances our self-worth and gives us many of the positive benefits of life itself—and believe me,

THE PRICE IS RIGHT

Frosty took out two small bronze plaques from my bag and handed them to Dan and Gary. They read aloud,

**THE REAL MEASURE OF ME IS NOT
WHAT I CAN DO COMPARED TO OTHERS
BUT WHAT I CAN DO
COMPARED TO MY BEST SELF**

"That's what we're talking about," Frosty said. "This exciting challenge of our BEST SELF, and we don't even know how good that can be!"

Gary spoke up and said, "Frosty, tell us the story of the eagle in the chicken pen. That one really helped me understand the potential I had and the choices I could make in my life that I didn't know about."

Donald was a young farmer who lived on a farm that spread out over the broad flatlands beneath a high cliff. One morning as he drove down the road next to the cliff, he noticed a nest like bundle of sticks lying by the side of the road. He stopped and walked over to it, and as he picked it up, he saw a baby eagle tucked into the broken nest. He looked up the high cliff, but couldn't see where the nest had fallen from. He placed the nest and the eaglet on a low ledge he could reach. The next day he found the nest by the road again with the baby eaglet in it. He picked up the eaglet and decided to take it back to his farmyard. When he arrived, he looked around for a place to put it. His eyes stopped at the chicken pen where all the baby chicks were. There was no roof on the pen, so the eaglet could get out when it was ready to fly. Thus, he decided this was the place and put the eaglet in with the young chicks. Time went by. The eaglet had now grown much larger than the young chickens in the pen.

One day the farmer's neighbor Roger came over to visit and noticed the eaglet in the chicken pen. He asked Don about it, and they both agreed it really didn't belong with the chickens and should start to fly as young eagles do. Even though there was no roof on the pen, the eaglet had remained there. Roger picked it up and took it outside the pen, held the eaglet high over his head, and gave him a toss into the air. The eaglet dropped to the ground and **shuffled back into the chicken pen**. They tried this maneuver several more times, with the same results. Always the eaglet **returned to the chicken pen**.

Several weeks later, Roger came back to visit Donald. This time he had a better idea on how to help the eaglet fly. He convinced Donald that all they had to do was to get it to spread its wings and it would then fly. The way to do this was to take the eaglet to the top of the cliff overlooking the farm and toss it off. Its wings would then spread out, and it would be able to fly. Donald agreed, so both men climbed the side of the cliff behind the farmyard, taking the eaglet with them. They came to the top of the cliff, the entire farm in view. Roger tossed the eaglet over the edge of the cliff. It fell like a rock toward the farmyard below. Both farmers looked in despair, cringing at the thought that they had made a big mistake and the eaglet was going to be crushed and die.

However, halfway down in its fall from the high cliff, the eaglet's wings opened and it went into a perfect glide. The two farmers looked at each other with big smiles on their faces as the young eagle circled through the air over the farmyard. However, as it neared the ground, they noticed it was **gliding directly toward the chicken pen.** The young eagle came closer and closer to the pen, preparing to settle on the ground with the chicks where it had been before. But at the last instant, it flapped its wings and started back up into the sky. Again and again the young eagle flapped its wings until **it soared high above the cliff and out of sight.**

"Did you get the message, Dan?" Frosty asked.

"I think so—regardless of its choice, the eagle would never be the same."

"That's exactly right," Frosty said. "The baby eagle had learned that it could fly; however, if it had chosen to go back to the chicken pen, it would not have been **the same eagle,** because now it knew it could fly. That's what I believe is going to happen to you. You will find that you are going to have another choice, a choice that right now you are learning about—then, like the eagle, regardless of which choice you make,

YOU WILL NEVER BE THE SAME.

Chapter 7

The Green Flash...

It was now late afternoon and the sun would be setting in the western sky in an hour or so.

Frosty looked at the guys. "Let's go for a jog on the beach past the big rock, and on the way back we can pick up some smaller rocks for our collections. We can be back here before sunset and start to barbecue our chicken and burgers for dinner along with fixing the salads and other good stuff. The main dinner attraction, however, will be the sunset and colorful afterglow."

Gary smiled and asked, "Will we see the green flash you told us about?"

"I'm not sure. Conditions have to be just right. It looks like a possibility as there are only a few clouds on the horizon and all the other clouds are scattered over the upper western sky. We'll just have to wait and see."

As they jogged on the beach by the big rock (which Frosty called the Gridiron), they could feel the slight breeze and cool air off the ocean. It was invigorating and uplifting for all of them.

They stopped on the way back and picked up some more rocks of various colors and shapes and returned to the cottage. They fixed a picnic dinner and put the barbecue meat on hold until they had seen the beautiful sunset.

Frosty spoke up as they stood by the railing looking to the west. "You can see a few clouds on the horizon, but they are not in line with the setting sun, so we may have a chance to see the green flash. However, this is a rare occurrence.

"It'll be several minutes before the sun starts to disappear, so let me try to explain what we're looking for. As the sun sets beyond the ocean and while the top of it is still visible, its multicolors start to disperse. We then see a red-orange color, a light yellow, and lastly, as the top rim of the sun disappears, a pale green color is visible. When atmospheric conditions are right and the horizon is clear, the last color, a light blue, which our eyes cannot distinguish, blends with the green and suddenly a brilliant emerald green flash appears for several seconds. It's spectacular! That's what we hope to see. It's going to come fast, so keep your eyes open."

The sun was now setting and as the top of it disappeared beyond the ocean, they could see the red-orange, yellow, and as it went out of sight, a light green color —

BUT... NO GREEN FLASH!

The light green remained on the horizon for a short time. The colors then blended into a reddish-orange on the nearby clouds, reflecting up into the western sky. The ocean turned a shiny, goldenrod color. It was a radiant sunset, but they hadn't seen the green flash. However, the changing, colorful sky was just beginning.

Gary, Dan, and Frosty moved their deck chairs back to the patio table, barbecued the main course meat, and enjoyed the delightful dinner while watching the multicolored afterglow of the sunset.

Frosty asked Gary and Dan, "How bout a popsicle?"

"Popsicles!" said Dan. "I haven't had one of those since I was a kid."

"You know, we need to keep part of that kid in us. Real joy comes when we continue to share that childlike excitement in our lives—not childishness, but genuine childlike enthusiasm. Far too many people lose this quality, and they become callused and indifferent toward many of the natural highs in life. Believe me, it makes us years younger and not years older.

"When I was a little guy, my dad owned a drugstore. Near the front of the store were freezers for ice cream, popsicles, and other frozen treats. Dad would bring popsicles home often. Our family and grandkids have really liked them over the years, so we always keep a supply of them. In fact, I would even get them for our football team periodically during the season when we would take a practice break. It was a great change of pace."

Frosty went to the kitchen and brought out a box of mixed flavors. Dan and Gary had their first popsicle in a long time as they continued to enjoy the afterglow's changing scenes.

"We're enjoying a colorful natural high right now," Frosty said. "And there are many more all around us. What are some others you can think of?"

Gary removed his popsicle from his mouth. "The sights and sounds of ocean waves, snowcapped mountains and hidden lakes, an illuminating sunrise, or a crackling bonfire on the beach."

"What are some other natural highs in our daily lives?"

Dan answered, "No traffic on our commute, a front row parking place at work, and a hot cup of coffee and favorite doughnut on my desk."

Gary continued, "A challenging workout, hearty laughter with good friends, my kids running out to meet me with hugs as I get home, and a special dinner with my wife at our favorite restaurant."

Dan spoke up, "A round of golf with a good friend, hearing one of your favorite songs on the radio, a long hot shower, and would you believe, no waiting in the checkout line."

Frosty clapped his hands. "These are all great! Notice that they are from different experiences.

There are so many more of them all around us. They are like the acre of diamonds. People just don't think of them as a high, but when they do, their lives are enriched."

Dan looked thoughtful. "Frosty, we've been together for less then a day, and it's been great! You are so enthusiastic, upbeat, and have such a good sense of humor. I feel good just being with you! The empty cup story has really made sense to me, and believe me, I am trying to empty my cup so I can fill it with the RIGHT STUFF that can improve my life."

"I have my disappointing down times just like anyone else," Frosty said. "Life in many instances is not fair. It's a series of ups and downs, and the way we respond is based on the attitude we choose.

OUR ATTITUDE NOT ONLY AFFECTS US, BUT EVERYONE AROUND US

"When we look for the worst in any situation, we can easily find it. However, when we look for the best, we can also find it, overcome the downers, and bounce back in a resilient and positive manner. We all need affirming and encouraging support to be able to do this. I have been blessed through my faith, my loving wife, Donna, my family, and other close relationships to have that support and in turn be able to support others—**it's a double win!**"

Frosty reached in the blue sports bag and brought out a peanut butter jar that was half full of small light and dark beans with an English walnut on top of them.

"This is an excellent example of what we've been talking about. The jar represents the place in our lives where we live and work. The beans represent the positive and negative stuff in our lives, and the nut represents us as a person—we are all a little nutty at times."

Dan and Gary laughed.

"When things are going well in our lives, we feel good and upbeat and on top of things, like the nut is right now. However when we encounter the negative and stressful stuff which happens to us in some ways every day, we can easily get down on ourselves. Psychologists say we have a minimum of seven disappointmenta day."

Frosty turned the jar upside down. Now the nut was on the bottom, underneath all the beans.

"Now we find out who we really are—we can gripe, complain, and blame others, become depressed and stay there, playing the "Poor Me" game, or we can respond in a another way through a optimistic attitude through our faith, and support from others. We can then become proactive and rise to the top."

Frosty shook the jar up and down, and the nut worked its way back to the top. He did it again, turning the jar upside down and shaking it, and the nut came back to the top. "I can do this a hundred times and it always comes back to the top. Proverbs 24:16 paraphrased says it this way, '*A person with character falls at times in his life but always rises again. A ruthless person stumbles and falls with anger and resentment during troubled times and fails to rise.*'"

"The bottom line is:

YOU CAN'T KEEP A GOOD PERSON DOWN

"Our enthusiasm for life is the key," Frosty said. "The word *enthusiasm* actually comes from the Greek and means the power of God within us. The difference between enthusiasm and faith is very slight. It is the strong positive attitude that generates from within. Webster's dictionary has many definitions and synonyms for enthusiasm. Here are a few: belief, spirit, passion, optimism, confidence, eagerness, vigor, excitement, energy, and intensity. It is actually all of these, and they add up to a—

REAL ZEST FOR LIFE!

"We can't be all these qualities, but we can be some of them, and that is what makes the difference in our lives."

Both men seemed to be connecting with this concept.

"Change takes time. The key is having the desire to change, and that's what the empty cup is all about. However, forming positive new habits isn't easy—they are like cobwebs at first and are easily swept away. But by persisting with meaningful repetition, you'll see these habits become like steel cables that support you in your new lifestyle.

"Dan, so many people just don't enjoy life. They look at it as one struggle after another. Don't get me wrong—we all have challenges and negative experiences every day, but our attitude toward them is what really counts. There are people who look at their week like this: Blue Monday, Hump Wednesday, and Thank God It's Friday.

"Many times their weekend is ho-hum, and they start over again the next week—the grind continues. Life is dull to dull people, and life is interesting to interesting people. You can't just have a good day like everybody says."

Gary chimed in,

"YOU HAVE TO MAKE IT A GOOD DAY!"

"I've really learned to do this," Gary said, "and it has made all the difference in the world in my life..."

Frosty nodded. "That's right, it all has to do with the attitude we embrace for that day. Making it a good day is a choice, and now that you know your choice is a power, you can use it to **make your day.**

"Laughter is a big part of making it a good day. We need to learn to laugh easily and naturally. I'm not talking about jokes, television sitcoms, the movies, or laughing at others. So much of this is negative put-down laughter. We need to learn to laugh with others, not at them. We should especially learn to laugh at ourselves. Most people take themselves far too seriously. We'll talk about this more later, but for now let's just enjoy the afterglow!"

As the afterglow turned into twilight, the sky darkened and stars started to appear. The three of us cleaned up dinner and moved into the cottage.

WE DON'T HAVE A GOOD DAY; WE MAKE IT A GOOD DAY!

Chapter 8

The Edge...

The coolness of the evening air made it feel good to be inside the cottage. The guys built a fire in the large stone fireplace, and it soon started crackling and burning brightly. They settled down on the comfortable couch and easy chairs in front of the fire.

On a small table in front of them, Frosty put the four red model cars in a circle and the blue one in the middle with the small wheelbarrow off to the side, the same way that he had done on the sundeck.

"Let's start our evening by doing our second one-minute drill. Look at your page with the sixteen-square grid. You've done it once. Let's see if you can find any more squares this time."

Dan and Gary did the drill and wrote the number of squares they found on the page.

"Let's see how we're doing."

"I got twenty-two both times," Dan said.

"I got twenty-two the first time and twenty-six this time," Gary said.

"Okay. Gary, show Dan the other four you found."

Gary pointed them out to Dan.

Frosty said, "Notice that we didn't change the sixteen squares on the outside; we just restructured them on the inside. That's what we're doing this weekend—restructuring ourselves on the inside. Our outside actions will change accordingly. We'll do this drill again later."

Dan said, "You mean there are more than twenty-six?"

Frosty smiled. "Let's just wait and see."

He handed Dan and Gary a diagram of the two models of winning.

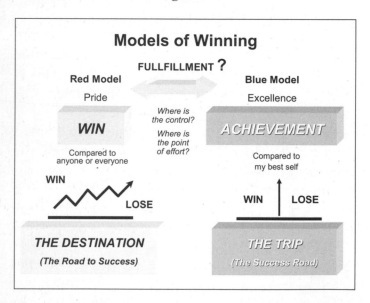

Models of Winning

FULLFILLMENT **?**

Red Model

Pride

WIN

Compared to
anyone or everyone

Where is
the control?

Where is
the point
of effort?

Blue Model

Excellence

ACHIEVEMENT

Compared to
my best self

WIN ⋀⋁⋀⋁⋀ LOSE

WIN | LOSE

THE DESTINATION

(The Road to Success)

THE TRIP

(The Success Road)

"There are big differences in the two models of winning. As you begin to learn, understand, and buy into the Blue Model and start to drive the Blue Car on the Success Road, exciting things begin to happen:

- you have more fun and fulfillment in the competitive arena.

- you achieve new levels of **EXCELLENCE BY EXPERIENCING THE DOUBLE WIN**

- you find a new awareness of personal worth in your life.

"The pay value is BIG TIME. For now you know that —

WINNING IS NOT SOMETHING YOU GET; IT IS SOMEONE YOU BECOME

"As we've been talking about," Frosty said, "these cars are very different. They have different engines and travel on two different roads. Remember, the red model sees winning as the goal at the end of the road; the blue model sees winning as a by-product of achievement—for the goal isn't the end of the road; *it is the road.*"

Gary nodded and said to Dan, "When I really understood this and saw the pay value it had, I bought into the blue car model and wanted to learn how to drive it on the success road. Frosty, share with Dan your poem, *The Enemy We Face.*"

Gary continued, "It was another thought pattern that helped me understand the blue car and relish the excitement of the competitive experience.

Frosty began "It goes something like this—no, it goes exactly like this."

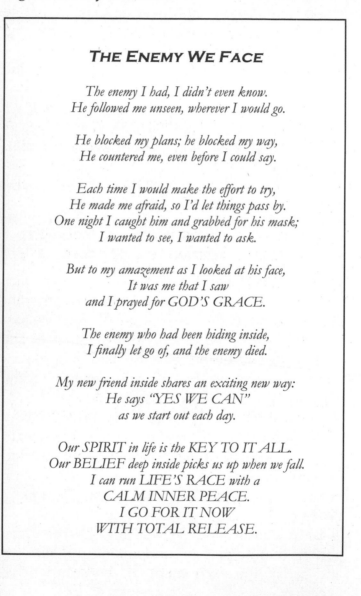

THE ENEMY WE FACE

The enemy I had, I didn't even know.
He followed me unseen, wherever I would go.

He blocked my plans; he blocked my way,
He countered me, even before I could say.

Each time I would make the effort to try,
He made me afraid, so I'd let things pass by.
One night I caught him and grabbed for his mask;
I wanted to see, I wanted to ask.

But to my amazement as I looked at his face,
It was me that I saw
and I prayed for GOD'S GRACE.

The enemy who had been hiding inside,
I finally let go of, and the enemy died.

My new friend inside shares an exciting new way:
He says "YES WE CAN"
as we start out each day.

Our SPIRIT in life is the KEY TO IT ALL.
Our BELIEF deep inside picks us up when we fall.
I can run LIFE'S RACE with a
CALM INNER PEACE.
I GO FOR IT NOW
WITH TOTAL RELEASE.

Dan responded right away. "The first part of the poem is what I've been like for as long as I can remember! I didn't know who my enemy was. Now that I do, the rest of the poem will help me to let go of the enemy and embrace a new—

YES, I CAN' ATTITUDE

Frosty continued, "Once we understand the vital importance of becoming our own good friend and learn to develop that Yes I Can belief in ourselves, the game of life changes dramatically in a positive direction."

"Here is a great concept – an action behavior model that will really get you started in that direction. It's called the Potential-Performance Gap [1]"

Gary instantly responded "This was a big momentum–builder for me when I started to drive the Blue Car on the Success Road."

I handed both Gary and Dan a copy.

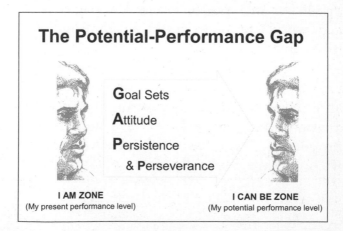

The Potential-Performance Gap

Goal Sets

Attitude

Persistence

& Perseverance

I AM ZONE
(My present performance level)

I CAN BE ZONE
(My potential performance level)

"The person on the left represents who we are right now – the **I Am Zone**. It is our present performance level in the eight key areas of our life (physical, mental, social, spiritual, family, financial, professional, and personal). The person on the right represents the **I Can Be Zone**. It is the potential possibilities for us in each of the eight areas. All of us have a GAP between what we are right now and what we can become. The real game in life is

ME VS. BEST SELF,
NOT ME VS. THE WORLD

We don't really know how great that can be. That's what really makes this game such an exciting challenge."

"The key to closing the GAP is in the GAP acronym itself."

G – is for **Goalsets** that come from our dreams, visions, and desires. These motivate us and generate energy that transfers into momentum in raising our performance level and can be a powerful force in building confidence and self worth.

A – is for **Attitude** – our habit of thought. We need to continue to build new positive attitudes in our daily lives through encouraging affirmations. These become a self-fulfilling prophecy for whether we think we can or think we can't – we're usually right.

P – is for **Persistence** and **Perseverance**. These develop our mental toughness and help us build our character into the person we really can be.

"When we continually apply this action behavior model of the GAP in our life we will reach higher performance levels that we didn't realize we could.

"The byproduct of this is we will have more fun and fulfillment in our daily lives and we will start feeling a new confidence in ourselves that we haven't had before, for

WHEN WE FEEL GOOD
ABOUT OURSELVES,
WE PRODUCE GOOD RESULTS

"Now let's take this a step further. Let's have a coin toss like we do to start a football game. The winner of the toss gets the choice of several options."

Frosty pulled out a quarter and got ready for the flip. I looked at Dan. "You call it."

"I'll take heads."

While the coin was in the air, Gary called out, "The EDGE!"

Frosty caught the coin in one hand and instead of turning it over flat on the back of his opposite hand, as is often done, he held it between his fingers so that neither the head nor the tail was up, but rather the edge of the coin.

"Gary, your call wins. It's the EDGE."

"Wait a minute," Dan gasped, "that isn't the way to do it! It's either heads or tails."

"You mean the EDGE can't win?" I asked.

"I've never heard of the edge winning."

"In a coin flip, you're right," Frosty said. "But we're not talking about a simple game of chance like a coin flip. We're going to talk about the third side of a coin—the side that most people don't know about or even realize is a side! We're talking about the EDGE. That small edge that encircles the entire coin really can make a big difference. Not in a coin flip, but in our lives.

"Competitors in any field talk about THE EDGE. Some have called it the winning edge; others have called it the competitive edge. Regardless of what you call it, THE EDGE is what makes the difference in your performance in any walk of life. This is WHAT THE BEST IS ALL ABOUT. Let's look at it from three different points of view, like the three sides of the coin that relate directly to the word BEST."

Dan and Gary settled into their seats.

"First off," Frosty began, "let's talk about the side of the coin that most people choose when we talk about best—that is, BEING THE BEST. We discussed the 'number one or no one' idea before, but let's look again from the view of the three-sided coin. People who choose this side of the coin talk about, think about, and go about—with all their time, talents, and efforts—trying to be number one in whatever they do. To measure this, they continually play the comparison game and are always searching for that road to success. The fallacy of this way of thinking is, as I said before, that we can't really control being number one. This side of the coin does not give you the edge. In fact, you really *lose* the edge. Being the best in anything is actually a by-product of the competitive experience, which most people don't understand. It is the result of a combination of various factors, and one of the most important ones is not defeating ourselves.

"The second side of the coin and the second view of best is DOING OUR BEST. We need to realize that doing our best is more important than being the best, because we are now focusing on our real competition: ourselves. As I shared in the poem, we can put our energy and efforts where they belong—on ourselves, where they can have the greatest effect on our performance. In the many diverse competitive areas of our lives, most of the time WE BEAT OURSELVES. We are out of focus and concentrating on the wrong target—our opponents. We cannot control them, but we can control ourselves, and when we really come to understand and believe this, WE WILL ADJUST THE WAY WE COMPETE. That's really important. We now focus on key targets we can hit. When we do this, our concentration and confidence are dramatically increased, thereby raising our level of performance. I realize there are times when we are defeated on a scoreboard or in a business situation by an outstanding performance from our opponent. However, a high percentage of the time, we actually beat ourselves through our own errors in judgment, basic mistakes, and improper use of our efforts.

"Studies of thousands of competitive situations document this fact. It's called the **60-30–10 Rule**. Sixty percent of the time we actually beat ourselves. Thirty percent of the time our opponent or competitors perform at a higher level and ten percent momentum is a key factor. With meaningful repetition and a directed focus on what we can control, we lower that sixty percent considerably. As a result, many times we gain the momentum. This puts us in control of a higher percentage of our performance in the competitive arena. We are then able to be at or near our best and be the best more of the time."

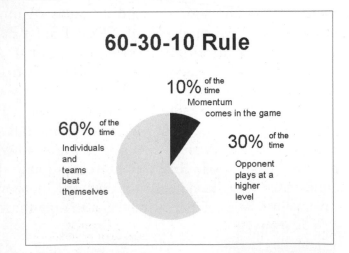

Frosty brought out a different chart. "There is another rule, the 20/80 rule, that says 20 percent of what we do produces 80 percent of the results. Too many people don't know what the 20 percent is that controls 80 percent of their performance. They focus on things that are out of their control or spend too much time on things that are insignificant. Each one of us needs to look at what we are doing and determine the key fundamentals and systems that really make a difference. We should then spend the majority of our time there. When we zero in on the key performance fundamentals and systems of a particular situation, we are now working on that 20 percent that really controls the level of that 80 percent of our performance. It's like changing our aim from long range, out-of-focus targets to short range, clearly defined ones. We now zero in on the bull's-eye, aim, and fire away. When we do this, our performance improves remarkably—that is, **if we aim before we fire.**

The 20/80 Rule

20% of what we do produces 80% of the results

20%

80%

80%

20%

The other 80% of what we do produces only 20% of the results

What We Do

Results
(High Level Performance)

"People who fire before they aim shoot from the hip and most of the time never come close to the bull's-eye. The key to reaching excellence on a consistent basis is to keep shooting at those bull's-eyes of our own specific targets and to be sure we aim before we fire. When we do this, we put ourselves in a position where being the best can become a bona fide by-product.

"The key questions are 'What is our best?' and 'How do we bring out our best?' The first thing we need to realize is that we can usually do much better than we think we can."

Dan and Gary nodded in unison.

"Potential is difficult to measure," Frosty said. "There are various tests: intelligence, fitness, skill, and other potential tests relating to specific performance.

"However there is another intangible quality in all of us that has far surpassed the results of these tests. That quality is an inner drive, a powerful drive, just waiting to be tapped. When it's tapped, we become truly motivated and shift into another gear we didn't realize we had. Success in anything in life is largely mental—not mental intelligence but mental attitude and mental toughness. Both of these are essential ingredients for doing our best.

"Our attitude, which is our habit of thought, is one of the keys to unlocking our potential. People live and die every day because of their attitudes and don't even know it. A winning attitude has to be learned; it doesn't just happen.

We must work to develop positive ideals that really do make a difference in our ability to do our best. This attitude constantly accents our strengths rather than our weaknesses, our desires rather than our fears. Weaknesses are changed into areas to improve—and improve we do! It's that dynamic spirit in our heart and soul that says, 'I can...I will...I must—regardless of the odds. I will get the job done within the letter and the spirit of the rules.'"

Frosty looked directly at Dan. "Even after understanding this view of doing our best, most of the time we still don't do it. Even though our focus is right and we apply the basic fundamentals of success, we still don't do our best most of the time, and the reason is THE EDGE. It's that slight edge that makes all the difference in our performance. It's that third side of the coin. Most all of us know it and talk about it, though we really don't understand it and apply it. But when we do, exciting things start to happen that bring out the best in ourselves more often."

Dan rubbed his chin. "I still haven't gotten it. What is THE EDGE?"

"We're talking about the third side of the coin, the third definition of *best*—that is,

GIVING IT OUR BEST SHOT

"This is the one area we have the most control over. Most people consider doing your best and giving it your best shot as the same thing, but they're not.

"You see, when we don't do our best or as good as we think we should, we get down on ourselves very quickly. We become frustrated, self-critical, and lose confidence. All this leads to the fear of failure, and we end up actually trying too hard, which results in lower performance levels. When we concentrate on giving it our best shot, we just reload and keep aiming and firing, while adjusting and adapting ourselves to each changing situation."

Frosty continued. "Belief is one of God's greatest gifts. It gives us the courage and confidence to keep on giving our best shot over and over again. We can continually enjoy the challenge of the moment, the excitement of each opportunity, and the by-product is that our best will come out a higher percent of the time. This is where

THE EDGE IS—
IT'S IN THE PROCESS

"Here's a poem that puts these thoughts and ideas into action:"

THE MAN IN THE ARENA

THE MAN IN THE ARENA you will know,
By the type of CHARACTER he will show,

As his FACE is marked with blood and sweat.
He continues to battle with an eager mind-set.

Some men will fold
when they struggle with pride,
And they lose their desire and drop off to the side.

Others grow stronger overcoming their flaws,
Enjoying the challenge, and not the applause.

The thrill of the battle is the key,
Which brings our best that only God's sees.
Whether we Win or whether we Lose,
We experience a Joy that few people Choose.

THE MAN IN THE ARENA
THAT IS THE SPOT
SO GO FOR IT NOW AND—
GIVE IT YOUR BEST SHOT!

Chapter 9

Let's Go to the Movies...

Frosty went to the back of the family room and rolled over a portable twenty-four-inch television set with a combination VCR/DVD player.

"We're going to the movie tonight, so just hang loose for a few minutes."

He went to the kitchen, microwaved two bags of popcorn, and brought it and some sodas back to the small table. Gary and Dan smiled and dug in.

"I've always liked to use different ways to communicate ideas, information, principles, and values," Frosty said. "Since we are such an extremely visual society, edited movie clips are an excellent way to do this. Our football team really likes these and relates to them Big Time. In fact, they bring video clips from movies they've seen that relate to the qualities we embrace on our team. They really enjoy them and can see the RIGHT STUFF in action. It raises their learning to Level 5, and I believe it can do that for you too."

Gary interjected, "Do you have one on the worm and alcohol?"

All three men laughed.

"We're going to watch three classic videos of the two different models of winning and leadership. The first is about a basketball coach and is from the movie *Hoosiers*."

Both Gary and Dan had seen it several times, so they remembered the story line.

"*Hoosiers* was recognized as the top motivational sports film of the twentieth century. We're going to see a clip from it beginning at the regional finals of the state tournament playoffs. As you remember, all the schools in Indiana were in the same classification. The smallest schools had to compete with the largest ones in the state.

Frosty turned on the video.

"The scene starts with Hickory High School, the small school team, getting off the bus and going into the gymnasium to play against one of the state's big school powerhouses. The scene shifts to the locker room and the last few minutes before the game. Their coach (played by Gene Hackman) gives his motivating pregame talk. The atmosphere is tense and the players are nervous. As the coach begins, all eyes are riveted on him. He talks about focusing on this game and no other. Play and focus in the NOW. He then goes on to say, 'Forget about the big crowd, the size of the school, their fancy uniforms. Remember what got us here.

Focus on the fundamentals and our systems of play that we've gone over time after time.' The coach's key idea then comes when he says, 'Most importantly, don't let yourself get caught up in thinking about winning or losing this game.' If you put your effort and concentration into playing to your potential to be the best you can be, I don't care what the scoreboard says at the end of the game. In my book, you will be winners.'"

"These young players wanted to win so bad they could taste it, and yet inside they had to deal with the intimidation, pressure, and the large crowd favoring the big school team. Belief in the coach's pregame talk calmed their fears and focused them on what they could do and what they could control. When the coach finished his talk, it was silent in the locker room. Then in a few moments one of the team players started to clap. The other players looked at him and then started clapping in unison, getting progressively louder and louder. They had been empowered with confidence and positive energy, and the entire team was now resolved and ready to give their best shot with no fear.

"The game goes down to the final few seconds, and a small backup player, playing for a starter who fouled out, was fouled with his team behind by one point. He got two free throws. He made the first one, tying the game. Before the second shot, an opposing player walked by and tried to psych him out with negative trash talk. His own teammate then affirmed and encouraged him. He shot the second shot, it bounced off the back rim, and went in. The crowd went wild—they had won the game and went on to win the state tournament.

Frosty shut off the video and said "The key to the team's outstanding performance was their attitude, positive mind-set, focusing on what they could control, and giving their best shot over and over again, which gave them the edge that really made the difference."

Both Gary and Dan really enjoyed the video and wrote the key points in their playbooks. While they had seen the movie some time ago, they had never looked at it from this point of view, and they recognized the powerful influence of positive coaching.

"The second movie clip we're going to watch is about two different coaching styles (red car vs. blue car). It's from the original movie of *The Mighty Ducks*." Neither Gary nor Dan had seen the movie.

Frosty turns on the video.

"It starts with a flashback on Gordon Bombay, a young coach (played by Emilio Estevez), when he was a little guy playing peewee hockey. His older coach was a red car coach who not only believed that winning was everything, but that winning was *the only thing* for him and his team. Fear of failure was his prime motivator. As time expires, Gordon gets a penalty shot that could tie the game and send it into overtime. The coach takes him by the shoulders, looks into his eyes, and says, 'It's up to you, Gordon. If you miss this shot, you're not just letting your team down, you're letting me down too. Remember, it's not worth playing if you can't win.' Gordon skates towards the net, one-on-one with the goalie. He shoots and the puck hits the metal bar on the side of the net and bounces away. He feels that he lost the game. He drops to his knees on the ice and looks at his coach. The coach turns away in disgust and won't even look at the young boy, for he was a loser.

"This attitude stayed in Gordon's subconscious mind as he grew up. He was afraid to fail at anything and become overly aggressive to prove himself worthy. He did become a good hockey player, then went on to law school and became a lawyer. But still this belittling negative attitude stayed with him over the years. He ended up coaching a young hockey team. His team was inexperienced and not very talented—in fact some of them could hardly skate and were not given a chance to even win a game.

"Gordon had witnessed the adverse effects his former red car coach had on him and the negative impact it had on his life. He had recently become friends with an older sportsman whom he genuinely respected and had a positive influence on his life. This man became his mentor and helped him let go of the many negative thought patterns of the past that had affected his self-image.

"By doing this, he was able to change his own life attitude in a positive way, learning how to think and feel good about himself and his associates. His new coaching style was positive and upbeat, and he affirmed and encouraged his young team consistently. His attitude along with his knowledge of hockey turned his ragtag team into contenders. They ended up playing for the championship against the old red car coach he had played for years ago, the very coach who had considered Gordon a loser.

"The game goes down to the final seconds with the score tied. One of Gordon's players is fouled on a breakaway and receives a penalty shot that could win the game. The same player will take the penalty shot. Gordon puts his hand on the boy's shoulder and looks him in the eye, much like his older red car coach had done years before—only this time it's totally different. He asks the young boy if he has been practicing his triple-deek move to score a goal. The boy says he has, and the coach tells him he's all set. He may make it, and he may not. The thing that matters is how far the team has come and how much fun they've had. 'No one thought our team would be playing for the championship,' Coach says. Coach Bombay reiterates the triple-deek move and tells the young player to take his best shot and that he believes in him whether he makes it or not.

"This coach-player talk seems to have calmed the young boy's fears and has given him renewed confidence. His team encourages him as he skates toward the goal. The crowd cheers loudly. He does his triple-deek move and scores the winning goal! His coach, team, and all the parents and fans run onto the ice and embrace the team. The opposing red-car coach looks at his team in anger and disgust, and they're fearful for they know they'll be punished for losing."

Frosty turns off the video and Dan and Gary took more notes in their playbooks. These two videos about life lessons were very impressive. They had never thought about the lessons they had learned from them and the effects of coaching leadership on the performance and lives of their players.

Frosty continued, "Red car ROAD TO SUCCESS people are all around us. They are very self-oriented. They are outwardly directed people who take their cues and develop their value systems and lifestyles from the models they see: their peers, loose-cannon TV personalities, radio, movies, the Internet, and the professional world. They then become their own self-fulfilling prophesy. They are number one...or no one.

"This road to success makes winning a mirage, a vivid illusion that disappears soon after you arrive. Fame is very fragile and fleeting. Most people don't even remember who won the World Series or Super Bowl just a few years ago."

Gary and Dan both nodded in agreement.

"They key thing about the red model of winning is that it has, in reality, produced very *few* winners. That is, people who think and feel good about themselves in the competitive arena and in their daily lives. They are robbed of winning because it's all based on the outcome. They may have championship rings to wear, but they never experience the true joy of the trip, and when it was over, they wondered where it led them."

Dan jumped in. "But I always thought positive type people were actually unrealistic and viewed life through rose-colored glasses. We live in a negative world, and we need to be tough to stay on the road to success to survive and win."

Frosty shook his head. "**Dan, it's more then surviving to win. You can be tough and optimistic at the same time**. A tough-minded optimist takes ordinary things and makes something out of them. He enjoys and experiences success in many new ways.

"Red car ROAD TO SUCCESS people may be successful on the outside. They can have well-paying jobs, be at various levels of leadership and prestige, have families, belong to social groups. However they are all missing the same thing—that enthusiasm, joy, and fulfillment in the competitive arena and in their daily lives.

"We all want to win in life, and sports can be a positive or negative influence. But only when we realize that each day we encounter many more negatives than positives. We must learn to respond to them in a resilient and positive manner to understand how to win in life. We live today—not yesterday or tomorrow. Many times, people focus on the regrets of yesterday and the potential fears of tomorrow, which robs them of the joy of today. We need to learn to really make *today* a good day, for that's where we live. It can be an exciting experience!

Frosty reached for the remote. "There's one more video clip I'd like you to see. It's from *Cool Runnings*, the story of a highly spirited Jamaican bobsled team."

Both Gary and Dan remembered seeing the movie and really enjoying it.

"I'm glad you've seen it," Frosty said, "but I want you to *really* pay attention for the pay value it has in making the most out of the competitive experience. We're going to watch a part near the end of the movie. It starts on the last day of time trials before the final day of competition.

"The rookie Jamaican team, in their ratty old sled, had come a long way and made their fastest downhill run on their last attempt, qualifying as one of the top eight teams. There was also an outside chance at an Olympic medal. The night before the final, the Jamaican bobsled driver Durese studied at photos of the downhill course they would race on. As he visualized every corner and turn from start to finish, his coach, played by John Candy, came into his room. Their conversation is one for the books.

Frosty turned on the video.

"The coach had been barred from competition some years before because of a cheating scandal and had been stripped of the two Olympic golds he had won. Durese asked him why he cheated, and the coach's reply was that he had to win. And once he won, he had to keep winning any way he could. Durese responded that the coach had won two gold medals—he had it all. The coach reiterated that he had made winning his life. He then shared from his heart that winning Olympic medals was great, but in all sincerity he believed that—

IF YOU'RE NOT ENOUGH WITHOUT THEM, YOU'LL NEVER BE ENOUGH WITH THEM!

"The young bobsled driver wanted to know when he would be ENOUGH. The coach then told him that he'd know when he crossed the finish line.

"The next day with high hopes the Jamaican team roared down the course with crowd cheering them on. The vast crowd had adopted them as their valiant underdogs and was rooting for them to win. They were going at top speeds when the steering mechanism of the sled faltered.

"They went out of control, flipping sideways, crashing into the wall, and sliding three hundred yards down the icy track before coming to a stop a short distance from the finish line. Bruised and battered, they slowly climbed out of their sled, picked it up, put it on their shoulders, and with character and class carried it across the finish line amid thunderous cheers, tears, and admiration from the thousands of spectators."

Frosty turned off the video, looked at Dan and Gary, and said "This Jamaican bobsled team represented what competition and winning in life is all about. They displayed what it is to give your BEST SHOT and follow through to the end, making the best of it regardless of the circumstances, regardless of the odds.

"The Jamaican bobsled team showed class in a special way. It's amazing to see how people respond to class. They are touched by this character trait, which is something we all inwardly admire. In many instances life is not fair. Everyone has challenges and obstacles to overcome, and when we see people respond in a resilient and positive manner, we all CHEER!

"Class is also displayed when we see an individual or team that is victorious unselfishly give credit to their competitors, their coaches or mentors, and their teammates—and we cheer when we see behavior like that! It's not 'look at me,' but 'look at *us*.'

"However, always lurking around the many positive actions and reactions are individuals and teams who have no class. They are selfish, ego-driven with negative self images These types of people are willing to do anything to win the medals and the glory that goes with them, so they cheat in sports, business, relationships, and even in families.

"Illegal performance-enhancing drugs are readily available today even though they are against the law, the medical code of ethics, and the governing rules of all sports organizations on every level. These drugs create quick physical fixes in body size, strength, speed, and stamina. The side effects include serious health problems later in life, but people don't seem to care and actually don't believe it will happen to them. They want to win *now*—so they cheat.

"They aren't eating their Wheaties; they're eating (or, rather, injecting in some cases) their Cheaties. Olympic athletes, professional athletes, and some college and high school athletes have been disqualified or stripped of their medals or trophies because of drug tests or other internal tests that determine illegal substances in the body.

"There are various other forms of cheating, but they all do the same thing, and this distorted mind-set undermines the very essence of human endeavor in sports, business, relationships, and families. The good news is that tighter standards and better testing procedures are being used and enforced at all levels to protect the integrity of the game.

Frosty looked at Dan and Gary. "I know it's getting fairly late, but I'd like us to do one more thing before we hit the sack. Nearly all top-level performers in any field have one thing in common. They all visualize the upcoming performance. They see themselves executing their task at their very best performance. They are very specific and they repeat it several times. They also visualize other life situations and have learned to enjoy the inspiration of these positive experiences. We're going to do one of these exercises, which will help end our first day together on a high note.

"I want you to lean back in your easy chairs, close your eyes, and get comfortable. I'll lead you through some deep breathing and some simple relaxation exercises. When I begin talking, I want you to visualize the pictures I'm sharing with you and let yourself flow as we go along. Follow me in your mind's eye on this adventurous journey."

THE MIND'S EYE

After several relaxing moments, Frosty began...

Tucked away in our subconscious mind is a picturesque vision—we see ourselves on a continually long trip across our vast nation. We are riding on a train. As we look out the big windows, we see cars whizzing by on the nearby highways, children waving at the crossings, cattle grazing on the distant hillsides, the flatlands and the valleys, the lakes and the rivers, the rolling hills and the rugged mountains, the small towns and the city skylines. The rich colors of fall, the snows of winter, the green of spring, and sunny summer.

But uppermost in our mind is our final destination. We know that on a certain day at a certain time we will arrive at the station and that will be it—happiness will abound. How restlessly we pace the aisles, cursing the minutes and counting the miles, waiting...waiting to get to the STATION.

The day finally arrives. Anticipation is high as we see ourselves pulling into the STATION. But wait—something is wrong. The STATION disappears right before our eyes.

The Station

We can't believe it. Then suddenly we realize that we have been deceiving ourselves all along. It really wasn't the STATION after all; the station was only an illusion in our mind's eye, and it has mysteriously vanished down the tracks and out of sight. It wasn't winning the championship, or getting the diploma, or becoming twenty-one, or the new car, or the new house, or getting the big promotion and pay raise. It wasn't really any one thing. The secret is that it is in the trip itself. The genuine joy of life is in the process of living. There is no one place to arrive at once and for all.

Psalm 118:24 says it all: "Today is the day the Lord has made, let us rejoice and be glad in it." We must really learn to do just that. It isn't that we just *have* a good day; we must learn to *make* it a good day. It isn't the burdens of today that cause us to lose our enthusiasm and zest for living. It is the regrets over yesterday and the fears of tomorrow. Regret and fear are twin thieves that will rob us of our joy today if we let them.

WE NEED TO CHOOSE TO MAKE EACH DAY A GOOD ONE

So stop pacing the aisles and counting the miles. Learn to enjoy the daily challenges in the marketplace. Take ordinary things in life and make something out of them: Develop a deeper relationship with family and friends, enjoy God's handiwork through His creation, hug a tree, go barefoot more often, walk more beaches, watch more sunsets (even more sunrises), eat more ice cream, sing more songs (even if we're off-key), and be sure to laugh more—especially with ourselves.

FOR LAUGHTER IS THE SUNSHINE OF OUR SOULS

Life should be lived as we go along. It's the
trip and not the destination that is important.
The goal is not at the end of the road—the
goal is the road. It's not counting the days—it's
making the days count. It's looking and seeing
more. It's listening and hearing more. It's loving
and sharing more. It's living each day of our
lives to the fullest; experiencing the genuine joy
of the trip.

After several minutes, Dan and Gary opened
their eyes and looked at the last embers of the
fire in front of them. They were relaxed and
mesmerized by the visualization session. It was
the first time they had experienced this.

Frosty was pleased that they had immersed
themselves in the exercise. "This mind's eye
visualization trip we took to the station helps
us to understand the essence of what our lives
are all about and how important it is to enjoy
the day by day experiences of life. I hope this
visualization session helped you to see that."

It was now midnight. As everyone turned in,
Dan commented,

"WE REALLY DID MAKE THIS A GREAT DAY!"

Chapter 10

Walk Your Talk...

Everyone was up early the next morning and went for a jog beyond the big rock. It was another beautiful, clear summer day. They stopped along the way and picked up some more colorful rocks for their collections and then took a swim in the waves of the oncoming tide.

They stopped on the beach just below the cottage. Frosty had left a bag of footballs in a large barrel near the steps.

"Let's play a game before breakfast!"

Frosty gave Gary and Dan three footballs and rolled the barrel out in the sand and marked off three lines—ten yards, twenty yards, and thirty yards from the barrel.

"We'll pass three footballs from each of the lines. When we hit the barrel on any of our passes, we get one point, and if when we pass the ball into the barrel we get three points."

Everyone started from thirty yards away. Gary hit the barrel with two of his passes. Dan missed on all three passes. Frosty hit the barrel with one of his passes. At twenty yards, Gary hit the barrel twice. Again, Dan missed them all, throwing the ball too hard and too low into the sand. Two of Frosty's passes went into the barrel. At ten yards, Gary made one in the barrel and hit it with one other. Frosty again made two in the barrel and hit it with the third. Dan was highly frustrated and tried too hard. He missed the barrel on his first two passes, throwing too high. He then turned and passed his last one toward the ocean. He was angry and upset.

The guys sat down on the sand, and Frosty looked at Dan. "This was a simple competitive game, and it became obvious that you were upset and frustrated when you weren't doing well, especially when you compared yourself to Gary and me. The harder you tried, the less accurate you became, and in the end you just gave up and tossed the last ball toward the ocean."

Dan shook his head in disappointment.

"It's amazing what competition brings out in us, isn't it?" Frosty said.

"Learning to compete in another way is not easy. It's not about beating Gary and I; it's about learning to make your best shot better by centering, refocusing, and affirming yourself. Negative thoughts and negative self-talk lower performance levels.

"We have a system for our football team in handling mistakes and low-level performance: 1) admit it, 2) learn from it, 3) FLUSH IT (the guys really like this part), 4) bounce back with affirmations and encouraging team talk, and

5) play in the now (it's the *next play* or our *next action* that really counts). It's important that we learn from and let go of mistakes. We are then ready to make our Best Shot better—even when it hasn't been very good."

Dan replied, "I really like that 'flush it' idea."

Gary and Frosty laughed with him.

"I do get upset when I compete and things start to go wrong. Your poem about the enemy we face is right on—it's me! But that's not how I want to be!"

Frosty squeezed Dan's shoulder. "That's okay, Dan. Many times we take two steps forward and then one back...sometimes even two back. Attitude changes take time and effort, and most people don't want to make the effort because they don't realize the powerful effect their attitude has on their lives and their performance. It's much easier to stay in the negative zone you're in rather than try to change.

"We continue to let outside forces affect our thinking, feeling, and action behavior because we're surrounded by so many so-called **thermometer-type people,** who are constantly controlled by outside conditions. We need to become **thermostat-type people**—we control the conditions from the inside out."

Frosty continued, "There is a big difference, Dan, when you realize that you have a choice you didn't know you had before—like the story of the eagle in the chicken pen. If the young eagle had chosen to go back to the chicken pen after he discovered he could fly, he would not have been the same because now he had a choice he didn't know he had before. He chose to fly into the unknown sky to become the eagle he really could be.

"You are going to have a similar, yet different, kind of choice because now you know that there is a different way to compete. You can continue to drive the red car on the road to success, which you are familiar with, or you can choose to drive the blue car on the success road, which seems risky and unknown."

The men returned to the cottage and fixed a hearty breakfast of juice, omelets, hotcakes, and coffee and ate it at the kitchen island.

They cleaned up and then went out to the sundeck and settled into their chairs under the umbrella.

As they sat down, Dan shared, "I got so frustrated and mad at myself on the beach, and I just don't want to be like that anymore."

Frosty nodded. "Frustration is part of life, and we continually need to adjust to it. Let me tell you one of the all-time frustrating and humorous experiences I had when I was a young coach…"

Years ago, I used to coach not only football, but also basketball, track, and baseball. This experience happened to me when I was coaching baseball in Iowa. We'd had several successful teams, and I had the opportunity to coach a college all-star team. The challenge was that we would be the only college team playing in a Class A professional league. My players were from Iowa, Minnesota, Wisconsin, and Illinois, and we were the underdog college team in this professional league. We practiced hard for several weeks and were ready to open the season. We played ten games and lost them all—we were 0–10. We weren't even close in any game. Two games were 18–3 and 15–1—it was very disheartening. We didn't play on the eleventh night because we were rained out, so I had a victory party. We weren't 0–11; we were still 0–10!

The team went to a pizza place and enjoyed ourselves. When we were through eating, I said to them, "We need to make some changes." Now that was the understatement of the year when we hadn't won a game and hadn't played very well. I looked at our three pitchers and said, "You three can play in the outfield— you're going to see what it's like to have those bombs come at you like has been happening the last ten nights. (Our pitchers had really been getting shelled. In fact, in the fifth game our infielders wore catcher's masks—now that's real confidence in your pitchers!)

John Stewart was our catcher from Iowa State. "John, you're going to pitch."

"Frosty, I oughtta pitch. I'm throwing it back harder than the pitchers are pitching it in there anyway."

"Okay, John. You can pitch." I changed every guy's position on the team.

Rog Shock was our third baseman from Illinois. "Rog, you're going to play first."

Here's what he said to me: "Frosty, I can't play first."

"Why not?"

"Because when I was a little kid, two years old, my mom and dad taped a little diamond in the kitchen. Dad would get on first, and I would be on third. Mom would hit a little puffball with her plastic bat to me. I'd pick it up and throw it to my dad on first. I was playing third base when I was two years old; then I played third in little league; then I played third in high school; and now I'm playing third at Illinois."

"Rog, first is just like third, but it's on the other side of the diamond."

He said, "But when I play, I get so psyched that I just play by habit."

"Don't worry, Rog, habits are the same." So he said okay.

The next night came, and we were all fired up. Our pitchers were in the outfield waving at the crowd. They were going to play a while because they weren't pitching and getting knocked off the mound, so they could chase all these hard-hit balls around. My catcher was throwing the ball in there at eight-plus miles per hour—he was really fired up! The game began and my catcher who was pitching struck out the side 1-2-3. We jogged off the field tied in the first inning! It was the first time in eleven games we'd ever been tied in the first inning (our pitchers had been getting shelled, allowing three to five runs).

We came up to bat in the bottom of the first. They were pitching their ace right-hander against us, and he struck us out 1-2-3. We were used to that!

Now the wild and confusing play happened. It was a classic in frustration. The first guy up in the second inning was their big left-handed clean-up hitter. My catcher, who had been pitching all fastballs, tried to throw him a curveball, and the guy hit a line drive straight down the first baseline. Rog, my third baseman who was now playing first, went high in the air, made a super play, didn't catch it, but the ball rolled off his glove about ten feet away from first base. Now all he had to do was pick up the ball and touch first base and the guy would be out by eighty feet. But all he could think about was throwing him out, so he pivoted around, cocked his arm, and went to fire it across the diamond. My center fielder, who was now playing third base, couldn't believe it! He started waving for Rog to run to the bag. Rog started waving at him to get on the bag. And as they were waving to each other, the hitter was coming down the first baseline. Everybody on the team just stood there and watched Rog—nobody could do anything.

All of a sudden, I came out of the dugout and yelled, "Rog—THE RUNNER!" He looked at the runner. Now, being a third baseman all he can think is, Run the guy down. So he started running at the runner. The runner started back to home.

Would you believe that we had this guy in a rundown play between first and home? It was the goofiest thing you ever saw! The ump let the play go, wondering, What kind of team is this? The crowd was going bananas. Our team was yelling, "Get him, Rog, get him!" Three or four relays back and forth and finally Rog chased the guy back toward home and dove to tag him with the ball. The runner slid in and the ump said, "You're safe!"

> Safe? I couldn't believe it. He hadn't even
> been to first base yet!

Gary and Dan laughed heartily.

"Frustration is part of everyday life. How we deal with it determines how we respond to the various situations we encounter. Here's a different version of the 20/80 Rule. Life is 20 percent what happens to us and 80 percent how we respond to it! It has everything to do with our attitude."

Frosty got out the red and blue cars again and placed them on the table as he had before.

"The 60-30-10 rule we talked about before is what really sells the blue car model of winning. It really helps us understand how many times we beat ourselves. It is the key to understanding where our point of effort should be to make our BEST SHOT the best we can. As a result, winning becomes a by-product.

"Learning to adjust to the many negative situations in life is key to helping us live up to our God-given potential. In football, the quarterback can call an audible on the line of scrimmage, changing the play to a better one to take advantage of a particular defensive alignment than the one called in the huddle. This adjustment many times can result in a successful play—even a touchdown.

"Many times it's the little things that make a big difference. We may be looking, but are we seeing? Like the sixteen-square grid we started with, when we opened up our awareness and made different adjustments, we found more squares.

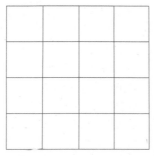

"In fact, there are actually thirty squares. The reason we don't see the last four is that they are three squares wide and three squares high, where the others are two-by–two, with the exception of the large one around the outside."

Gary and Dan looked at their grids again and were now able to see all thirty squares.

"We still have the same framework on the outside of the original sixteen," Frosty said, "but we now have connected them in new ways. This is the same way we make changes in our own lives from the inside out."

"We do a fun and challenging activity with our football team every Monday at our team meeting. It is in some ways like finding the thirty squares, for it challenges our players to recognize key differences in a short period of time. This carries over into the quick recognition of defensive and offensive formations in the game. The players look forward to this challenge. It's called Hocus Focus. Two cartoons that look very similar are placed side by side, but there are six differences between them. A few are obvious and some are subtle. We give the players thirty seconds to see how many they can find and then thirty seconds to talk with a teammate to see if together they can find all six. They really get good at this. Let's give it our best shot. Ready…go!

Find six differences in details between panels.

Hocus-Focus

By Bob Schroeter

Used by permission of the Kings Features Syndicate [1]

The guys looked carefully at the cartoons. At the end of the 30 seconds, Gary and Dan had each found four of them. Talking together for 30 seconds more, they found another one. [How did you the reader do?] The answers are in the End Notes at the end of the book.[2]

"Let's look at one more example of adjusting," Frosty said. "It happened on our first space flight to the moon. The monitoring system used by mission control was a large, oversized set of traffic signal lights.

"When the spaceship was on course, the GREEN light appeared. However, when it started to veer off course, the AMBER light would come on. Mission control would then adjust the spaceship back on course and the GREEN light would come back on. If the RED light came on, it was a MAYDAY signal that the spaceship was out of control and getting totally off course — they always made the proper adjustments and never let this happen.

"The interesting thing though about the entire flight was that the AMBER light was on over half the time, and *slight adjustments* had to be made to keep them on course with the GREEN light showing. The success of this spaceflight was determined by adjustments that were continually being made by mission control.

"The same is true in our individual lives. The key is learning to make the right adjustments, and it all starts with small ones."

Frosty handed Gary and Dan an outline of Blueprint for Life #1.

IT'S A CINCH BY THE INCH
AND HARD BY THE YARD!

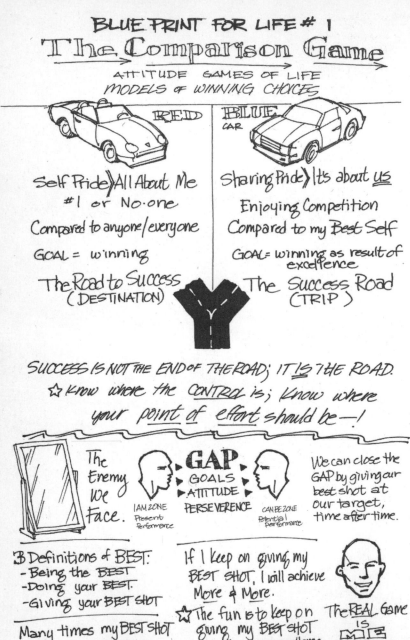

BLUE PRINT FOR LIFE # 1

The Comparison Game

ATTITUDE GAMES OF LIFE
MODELS of WINNING CHOICES

RED | **BLUE** CAR

Self Pride > All About Me | Sharing Pride > It's about us
#1 or No·one | Enjoying Competition
Compared to anyone/everyone | Compared to my Best Self
GOAL = winning | GOAL = winning as result of excellence
The Road to Success (DESTINATION) | The Success Road (TRIP)

SUCCESS IS NOT THE END OF THE ROAD; IT IS THE ROAD.
☆ Know where the CONTROL is; Know where your point of effort should be—!

The Enemy We Face. | **GAP** GOALS · ATTITUDE · PERSEVERENCE | We can close the GAP by giving our best shot at our target, time after time.

I AM ZONE Present Performance · PERSEVERENCE · CAN BE ZONE Potential Performance

3 Definitions of BEST:
- Being the BEST
- Doing your BEST
- Giving your BEST SHOT

If I keep on giving my BEST SHOT, I will achieve More & More.

Many times my BEST SHOT is not my best performance

☆ The fun is to keep on giving my BEST SHOT & I will achieve excellence and be the best more of the time! ☆

The REAL Game IS ME vs BEST SELF

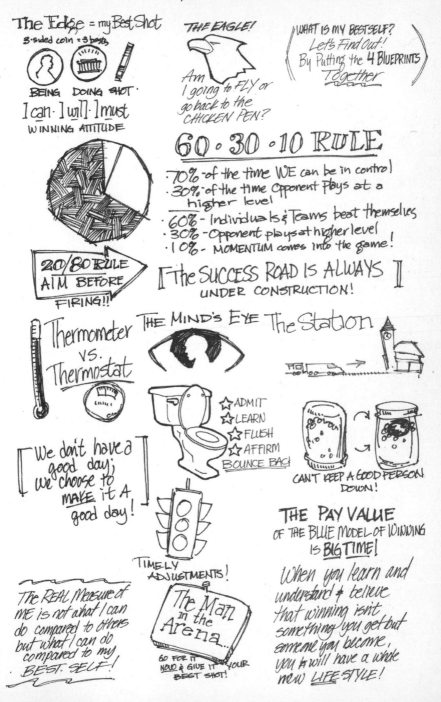

The Edge = my Best Shot

3-sided coin = 3 bests

BEING · DOING · SHOT

I can · I will · I must

WINNING ATTITUDE

THE EAGLE!

Am I going to FLY or go back to the CHICKEN PEN?

WHAT IS MY BEST SELF? Let's Find Out! By Putting the 4 BLUEPRINTS Together

60 · 30 · 10 RULE

- 70% of the time WE can be in control
- 30% of the time Opponent plays at a higher level
- 60% - Individuals & Teams beat themselves
- 30% - Opponent plays at higher level!
- 10% - MOMENTUM comes into the game!

20/80 RULE AIM BEFORE FIRING!!

The SUCCESS ROAD IS ALWAYS UNDER CONSTRUCTION!

Thermometer VS. Thermostat

THE MIND'S EYE   The Station

☆ ADMIT
☆ LEARN
☆ FLUSH
☆ AFFIRM
BOUNCE BACK!

We don't have a good day; we choose to MAKE it A good day!

CAN'T KEEP A GOOD PERSON DOWN!

TIMELY ADJUSTMENTS!

THE PAY VALUE OF THE BLUE MODEL OF WINNING IS BIG TIME!

When you learn and understand & believe that winning isn't something you get but someone you become, you will have a whole new LIFE STYLE!

The REAL Measure of ME is not what I can do compared to others but what I can do compared to my BEST SELF!

The Man in the Arena...

GO FOR IT NOW & GIVE IT YOUR BEST SHOT!

Chapter 11

Blueprint for Life #2: The Confidence Game

A large cruise ship was passing by a half mile away. The three of us got up and walked to the front of the sundeck and watched it for a short time until it sailed past the Gridiron rock.

Returning to their chairs, they resumed their discussion.

"We are now ready for Blueprint for Life #2," Frosty said.

THE CONFIDENCE GAME

"Confidence is contagious, and so is the lack of confidence. You can hear it, feel it, and see it in a person, team, or organization in a very short time. It is one of the most talked about qualities regarding success—peak performers in any field agree that confidence and belief are the essential ingredients for success.

"However, we need to understand what confidence really is—how to develop it within ourselves, with our family, our team, our organization, and then how to transfer it from one life situation to another."

Gary and Dan were paying close attention.

"We're not talking about cockiness, conceit, or arrogance; we're talking about that quality of positive assurance and self-esteem. It is believing that you can accomplish your desires and goals in life and overcome obstacles you encounter, then having the courage to go for it.

"There are two different theories on how to develop confidence. Some of these differences are very subtle, and others are very noticeable. The red car model of confidence is based on comparison success, and it stresses constructive and destructive criticism and varying degrees of fear motivation. The put-down game (blowing out others' candles so yours will shine brighter) is part of this. Proponents of this model believe that by doing this you become tough-minded by intimidating others, which thereby gives you an advantage in being successful.

"The blue model, based on achievement success, stresses affirmations plus encouragement and relationship motivation. The put-up game (lighting others' candles so we all shine brighter) is key—it is teamwork in action and gives confidence and respect to others on the SUCCESS ROAD even when the going is tough."

Frosty pointed toward the big rock. "Here's a good example of this."

Gary and Dan turned to look.

"Look at all the seagulls that are perched on and are flying around Gridiron Rock. They stay in this area the entire year. However there is another breed, the Northern Geese, who make their home in the upper U.S. and Canada and migrate south each year in the fall before winter sets in and lakes and ponds start freezing over.

"We see them flying in that familiar V formation. There is a reason they do this. By studying the geese, researchers have found that as each bird flaps its wings, it creates uplift for the trailing goose. By flying in a V formation, the whole flock adds 70 percent greater flying range than if each bird flew on its own.

"When the lead goose gets tired, it rotates back in the formation and another goose flies on the point. The geese also make their honking sound to support each other and to let them know they are in formation to keep up the speed."

Gary and Dan shook their heads. This was the first time they'd ever heard anything like this.

"This is a remarkable example of teamwork at its best," Frosty said. "By flying in formation and communicating with each other in an upbeat way, they perform at a higher level. They exemplify the true meaning of the acronym

TEAM–
TOGETHER EVERYONE ACHIEVES MORE

"It's synergy in action—the whole is greater than sum of its parts.

"We can all take a page from the geese's playbook about the blue car model of winning."

ITS' AMAZING HOW MUCH CAN BE ACCOMPLISHED WHEN NO ONE CARES WHO GETS THE CREDIT!

Gary and Dan both jotted this down in their playbooks.

"Here's another excellent example of the power of the put-up game," Frosty said.

> A high school football coach's team wasn't playing very well. In fact, they had lost most of their games during the season. They were a talented group of players who weren't playing up to their potential. It seemed they were just going through the motions. There didn't appear to be any team spirit or team morale.
>
> Early one week after losing another game, the coach stood off to the side of the field and just watched and listened to the players as they practiced. It didn't take long before he was able to see and hear what was going on. He was amazed that he hadn't noticed it before. His players were constantly putting each other down when they dropped passes, missed blocks or tackles, or busted assignments.
>
> Some of it was good-natured wisecracks, yet some of it was demeaning. No one really meant any harm, but it was obvious as the coach listened that this put-down stuff was

contributing to lack of team spirit and low morale.

He blew his whistle and had the entire team come and sit in the bleachers. Everyone remained silent for a few minutes. The coach then told them how he had listened from the sidelines the last half hour and heard how they talked to each other on the field. He had realized a problem they needed to know about.

They were playing a negative game with each other that they were not aware of. It was the put-down game. They were putting each other down time after time, whether degrading or in fun, and it had become a habit—team morale was low. The coach said, "We're going to play a new attitude game from now on called PUT UP or SHUT UP. In other words, if you can't encourage or affirm a teammate or yourself, don't say anything at all."

For the next several days at practice the players were very quiet. They actually didn't know or recognize how to put each other up!

The head coach and his staff made special efforts putting up and encouraging the players during their practice sessions. On the last day of practice before the next game the players who had been hearing put-ups regularly from their coaches started putting each other up. They had bought into the idea and really started to acknowledge good plays, second effort, and also encouraged each other when they didn't do well.

The spirit of the team, as well as their performance, increased big time, and the momentum they created helped them ignite team spirit to go on to win the rest of their games.

The coach hung a "PUT UP or SHUT UP" sign in the locker room. The players then made a habit of touching it as they went to the field.

The entire school picked up on the momentum of the football team, and the student council sponsored a PUT UP or SHUT UP week for the entire school, hanging colorful banners around the school. One of the best ones was:

SCORE A TOUCHDOWN TODAY— PUT UP SIX PEOPLE, INCLUDING YOURSELF!

Dan remarked, "The coach had some good insights in regard to his team's low morale and mediocre performance. His firm approach is what really turned his team into winners."

"That's right Dan," Frosty said. "The blue model uses a firm approach at various times. However, it is in the form of tough-minded optimism. It is friendly yet firm, much like the coach in his Put Up or Shut Up declaration to his team. **BELIEVE ME — THERE IS POSITIVE POWER IN THE PUT UP GAME.**

"Many people think of tough in a negative sense, such as being cold or rough. What the blue model is talking about is the upbeat side of tough, which is having the quality of being strong, or firm, flexible, yielding to force without breaking, resilient, and enduring.

"The blue model takes 'tough' one step further, adding optimism. This brings about actions to overcome obstacles and achieve desires and goal-sets. Optimism is self-fulfilling prophecy that says, 'Whether you think you can or think you can't, you're usually right!' Optimism dwells on what we want to happen, not what we don't want. It dwells on areas of strength and areas to improve on, not weaknesses; it thinks about desires rather than fears, because remember...

WE BECOME WHAT WE THINK ABOUT!

"Here's a story of an exciting playoff game some years ago that exemplifies this."

The outcome of the game came down to the last play—we were leading 28–27.

The opposing team had the ball on our thirty-five-yard line—third down and five yards to go—with only twenty seconds remaining in the game. Our starting cornerback had been injured and his backup Terry Hartman, who was a small guy—five foot nine, 155 pounds—was in the game in his place.

Our opponent had a strong running game featuring their All-American running back, who was six foot two, 220 pounds, fast, and powerful. He had already scored three touchdowns on long runs.

The crowd was standing and going bananas.

The ball was snapped—they ran an off tackle play they had scored on before with their powerful running back. He broke into the clear and was running for the winning touchdown.

Terry had run across the field at an angle from the other side and was able to get in front of the big runner on the ten-yard line. As the runner tried to cut back, Terry hit him hard with his shoulders, wrapped his arms around him, brought him to the ground, and laid on him on the ten-yard line as the game ended to secure the victory.

Our team stormed onto the field. The impact of the tackle had briefly knocked Terry out. He was just coming to as our team lifted him on their shoulders and carried him to the locker room. It was a mountaintop moment for all of us.

Gary and Dan had really been into the game story. Gary excitedly said, "What a great play your small defensive back made."

"It sure was, Gary. It represented that classic saying—

IT'S NOT THE SIZE OF THE DOG IN THE FIGHT; IT'S THE SIZE OF THE FIGHT IN THE DOG!

"It would have been easy for Terry to just dive in the air and try to hit this big runner from the side, avoiding full contact, but he didn't," Frosty said. He hit the powerful runner straight on and brought him down.

"The key question is, what put Terry's shoulders there to make this game-winning tackle? It wasn't muscle or bone, it wasn't size or strength—it was a big heart and a never-say-die spirit that says, 'I can, I will, I must—regardless of the odds.'

"It's this kind of courage, which we call guts, that we all admire when the little guy takes on the big guy and wins. Like the classics: David and Goliath, Gideon's 300 vs. the 135,000 Midianites, and Popeye and Bluto. We have a sign in our locker room that says—

WE FURNISH EVERYTHING
BUT GUTS

"For many years we have had players as well as coaches who had this kind of courage to make outstanding clutch plays and take calculated risks when the game was on the line regardless of the odds. Their belief in themselves, in our systems, and in each other made our best shot the BEST on many occasions."

Gary and Dan nodded.

"When you are tough-minded and optimistic, you are able to do these kinds of things. You can counter the negative stresses in your life and face challenges and difficulties with strength and determination and deal with frustration in a positive way.

"You deal with mistakes and low-level performance with the system we shared before—

1— ADMIT IT
2— LEARN FROM IT
3— FLUSH IT
4— POSITIVE SELF-TALK
5— BE READY TO PLAY IN THE NOW

SELF IMAGE

"The ability to think and believe like a tough-minded optimist is the high-energy fuel that powers the engine of the blue model car. It generates a peace, power, and joy that allow us to do exceedingly well in the many aspects of the game of life."

Gary and Dan wrote the key ideas we had just gone over in their playbook.

"Here's a special poem that says it so well," Frosty said. "Its consistent thought pattern of belief is the key to success in any field."

YOUR STATE OF MIND [1]

If you think you can, YOU CAN.
If you think you dare not, you don't.
If you think you can't, but really can—
It's almost a cinch you won't!

For out in this world you'll find
Success begins with a person's will,
It's all in your STATE OF MIND.

Many a game is lost
Before ever a play is run,
And many a coward falls
Before their work's begun.

Think big and your deeds will grow,
Think small and you'll fall behind.
Think you can and you will.
It's all in your STATE OF MIND.

If you think you're outclassed, you are.
You've got to think high to rise.
You've got to learn to be sure of yourself
Before you can ever win a prize.

Life's victories don't always go
To the stronger or smarter woman or man.
But sooner or later the person who wins
IS THE PERSON
WHO THINKS THEY CAN!

Gary said, "That poem really says it all."

"It sure does, it sure does" Frosty replied, "and the blue car model has learned to think like this and has more fun in the natural highs of life, looking for opportunities to affirm and encourage others.

"My wife, Donna, has a great saying for this. It's a paraphrase from Ecclesiastes 11:1:

CAST YOUR BREAD UPON THE WATERS AND IT WILL COME BACK WITH STRAWBERRY JAM

"As we inspire others—we become inspired!"

Gary responded "It sure sounds like your wife Donna drives a Blue Car on the Success Road."

Frosty smiled. "She sure does." He reached into the blue bag and gave Dan and Gary a desk plaque with the strawberry jam quote.

"It seems to me that most people drive a red car, but will also drive a blue car some of the time. Can't you drive both cars on this SUCCESS TRIP?" Dan asked.

"Look at it this way," Frosty said. "Let's say we all have two cars in our garage. Either two red, two blue, or one red and one blue. The driver of the two red cars would be relatively consistent with their "number one or no one attitude" and lifestyle choices traveling on the Road to Success. The driver of the two blue cars would be relatively consistent on their double-win lifestyle choices on the Success Road.

"However, if you drive the red car/blue car at different times, it will be very difficult for others to identify who you are due to the different mood swings and attitude differences of each model. Remember, you are traveling on two different roads. You really have to choose which car you are going to drive and which road you are traveling. The trip you take will be your choice of lifestyle."

Gary and Dan were focused on Frosty's words.

"The red model does acknowledge good performance at times and can appear in some ways similar to the blue model, yet criticism is the dominant quality used in life situations. It may be brash or subtle, but it is the key mindset (telling people what they shouldn't do and motivating through fear of failure).

"The blue model will also use a firm approach at times (tough love), however it always relates back to affirmations and encouragement (telling people what to do) to generate momentum.

Momentum is a powerful force that affects confidence and raises performance. People start responding to challenges and the overcoming of obstacles when they start pushing the positive buttons in themselves and others. This greatly enhances the feelings of self-worth, and the by-product is EXCELLENCE as they travel on the Success Road.

"By utilizing the blue car attitude and action tools, one is able to transfer confidence from one life situation to another.

AND THAT IS BIG TIME!

BY LIGHTING OTHERS' CANDLES WE ALL SHINE BRIGHTER

"One of the by-products of lighting others' candles," Frosty said, "is the DOUBLE WIN (bringing out the best in ourselves and others), which we have talked about before.

"This is directly related to CLASS. Class sees life as the ultimate game and knows how to play it. It encompasses our mind, body, and spirit and is concerned with the overall good. A person with class will reflect this by the choices he makes and the actions he takes in any given situation."

Gary responded, "I remember at our mountain breakaway, we talked about Steve Largent, the All Pro receiver and congressman, and John Wooden, the great UCLA basketball coach, as two prominent examples of class. Both of these men are highly respected and admired."

"That's right, Gary," Frosty said. "They are key role models. I have revised this article on CLASS, which shares many of its qualities in a special way. Read each quality of 'What is Class' carefully—think about it and see how it relates directly to the blue car model traveling on the success road."

Frosty handed a copy of Blueprint for Life #2 to each of them along with the poem 'What is Class.'

BLUE PRINT FOR LIFE # 2

The Confidence Game

ATTITUDE GAMES OF LIFE

LIFESTYLE CHOICES

RED CAR | **BLUE** CAR

THE PUT DOWN GAME

Belief that by putting others down you will show you are better.

THE PUT UP GAME

Belief that by putting others up we all perform at higher levels

CONFIDENCE AND BELIEF ARE ESSENTIAL INGREDIENTS FOR SUCCESS

WE **BECOME** *What We Think About!*

CONFIDENCE IS CONTAGIOUS AND SO IS LACK OF CONFIDENCE

FOOTBALL COACHES PUT UP OR SHUT UP GAME.

IT'S AMAZING HOW MUCH CAN BE ACCOMPLISHED WHEN NO ONE CARES WHO GETS THE CREDIT

Teamwork of the Northern Flying Geese:
- Fly together much farther
- Honk to support each other & to let flock know they are in formation to keep up the speed.

IT'S NOT ABOUT MATCH UPS — IT'S ABOUT PLAYING UP TO OUR POTENTIAL

WHAT PUT TERRY'S SHOULDERS THERE TO MAKE THE GAME SAVING TACKLE? IT'S WHAT'S INSIDE THAT COUNTS!

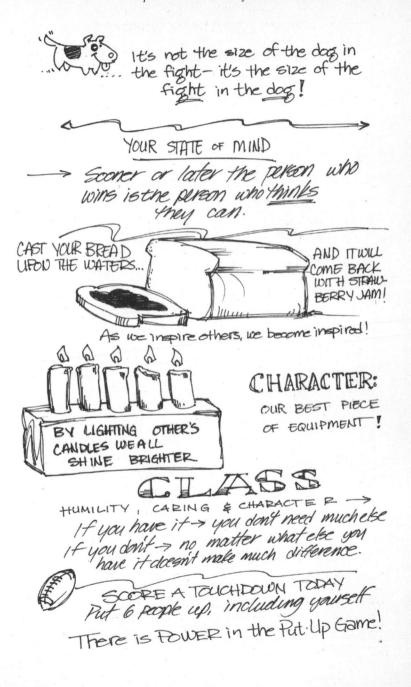

It's not the size of the dog in the fight – it's the size of the fight in the dog!

YOUR STATE OF MIND

→ Sooner or later the person who wins is the person who *thinks* they can.

CAST YOUR BREAD UPON THE WATERS... AND IT WILL COME BACK WITH STRAWBERRY JAM!

As we inspire others, we become inspired!

BY LIGHTING OTHER'S CANDLES WE ALL SHINE BRIGHTER.

CHARACTER:
OUR BEST PIECE OF EQUIPMENT !

CLASS
HUMILITY, CARING & CHARACTER →

If you have it → you don't need much else
If you don't → no matter what else you have it doesn't make much difference.

SCORE A TOUCHDOWN TODAY
Put 6 people up, including yourself
There is POWER in the Put-Up Game!

WHAT IS CLASS?[2]

Class is a special quality.
It is revealed through attitudes, actions, and reactions.

Class doesn't have to think about responses—
It just does it!

Class is respectful and considerate of others.
It brings out the best in them.

Class never tries to build itself up
by tearing others down.

Class never makes excuses—
It takes its lumps and learns from each experience.

Life in many instances is not fair,
yet class meets life's challenges head on
and responds in a resilient and positive manner.

Class loves the competitive experience.
The tougher the challenge, the better it is—
When the goin' gets tough—
Class gets it goin'.

Class has nothing to do with Status, Wealth, or Fame—
the greatest model of class in the history of mankind
was a CARPENTER.

Everyone is comfortable with a person who has class—
because they are comfortable with themselves.

If you have Class, you don't need much of anything else.
If you don't have it, no matter what else you have—
it doesn't make much difference

Chapter 12

Blueprint for Life #3:
The Challenge Game

The guys heard the cottage door open, and Cliff came through the sliding doors onto the sundeck.

"I had my sons bring me down this morning," he said. "They're going to beachcomb, boogie board, and swim for a while and then drive back. I'll ride to the airport with you tomorrow."

Cliff pulled up a chair and sat down.

Frosty said, "It's great to have you here with us, Cliff. We have just finished going over Blueprint for Life #2."

"Notice, guys, that Frosty didn't say *Redprint* #2!"

Both Gary and Dan smiled.

"The four blueprints for life you are learning about are the basis for our academy program," Cliff said. "When our students use the tools to build these blueprints, you see a noticeable positive difference in their lifestyle. The change for many is remarkable. However, it takes continued meaningful repetition in everyday situations to affect their choices and who they hang out with."

"Cliff will share with us more about the application of the blue car model in his academy program a little later," Frosty said. "We are now ready for

BLUEPRINT FOR LIFE #3:
THE CHALLENGE GAME

"We once again have the opportunity to use our power of choice on how we respond to life's many diverse situations," Frosty said. "We can choose to see them as either problems or challenges, and there is an important difference.

"Many people look at their lives as a continuous series of problems. This can become a self-fulfilling prophecy and cause a negative or troubled mind-set of doubtfulness and frustration. They start to lose hope and belief in themselves, which results in fear of failure or ability to succeed.

"Challenges, on the other hand, are an energizing, positive way to approach life's situations. This mind-set can stimulate and excite us to go for it without fear and enable us to give our BEST SHOT over and over again to overcome the obstacles we face.

"Today, too many people give up on things they want to accomplish or become because they didn't do it right away or as soon as they thought they should. Making the second effort and persevering over the obstacles are keys to accomplishing our visions, desires, and goal-sets, and many people quit way too soon. There are others, however, who were inspired by a coach, a mentor, a parent, or someone along the way to make that second, third, or fourth effort to accomplish their dreams and desires regardless of the odds."

Frosty looked at the guys. "There are blind golfers who shoot in the nineties, handicapped swimmers and riflemen who become champions, a one-legged football player who was voted the most inspirational athlete in America, and marathon wheelchair racers who push themselves beyond anything ever before to accomplish their goals. All of these people were inspired to make that extra effort—regardless of the odds.

"Winston Churchill, the great prime minister of England during WWII, gave an inspiring seven-word speech during the country's darkest hour. **Yes, I said seven words.** The speech lasted less than thirty seconds, yet it gave the entire country the courage to continue the war at a very discouraging time. The seven words were:

NEVER, NEVER, NEVER, NEVER, NEVER GIVE UP!

"A pound of inspiration is worth a ton of information," Frosty said.

"Many premed students who don't get accepted to medical school on their first or second attempt change tracks and pursue other professions or different branches of the medical field. They don't make the second effort to reach their vision and desire.

"Here's a splendid example of making the second effort from one of our former football players. Jeff Douglass was one of the captains of our football team in the early nineties. He was a fine player and an inspiring team leader."

Jeff was a good student and graduated premed. He applied to various medical schools around the country. He received the same response—not accepted. Jeff was put on second and third level of applications with little encouragement that he would be accepted.

The next year he volunteered and had the opportunity to work with an outstanding older physician who was slowly losing his eyesight. They developed an excellent rapport and respect for each other. Jeff actually became the eyes of the older doctor in many situations. Needless to say, at the end of that year, the older doctor helped open the doors to medical school for Jeff because of his belief in him.

Today Jeff is an outstanding doctor practicing in the Portland area.

It takes real courage for a person keep making efforts that don't seem to make any difference—to persevere when the odds seem against them. There are times, however, when a person needs to change direction due to factors beyond his control. This is where a mentor can be a real help in the decision-making process.

There is an inspiring book titled, *Courage Is a Three-Letter Word*. It's the word YES—Yes, I can; Yes, I will; Yes, I can say no (no to negative influence); Yes, I believe I can. It's the "Little Engine That Could" story over and over again.

"The key to this is being able to control our attitude during life's many ups and downs," Frosty said. "The tool for this is learning to control our **self-talk**. We need to use this simple yet powerful tool in a positive way, enabling us to counter negative self-talk. It's so easy to put ourselves and others down with negative talk when we become frustrated and don't succeed or do as well as we think we should have. We need to learn to develop positive self-talk with affirmations and encouragement. This motivates us to continue to go for it with our best shot. It can become a positive self-fulfilling prophecy:

WHETHER WE THINK WE CAN OR THINK WE CAN'T, WE'RE USUALLY RIGHT!

Dan said, "I don't remember talking to myself. I mean we really do talk to ourselves?"

Frosty smiled. "We don't always say it out loud. Many times it's just a thought pattern or feeling within us. It's like this morning, in our beach football pass game, when you were playing the red car comparison game by getting mad and putting yourself down. This contributed to your low-level performance. Positive self-talk would improve focus and performance."

Cliff spoke up, "I deal with a lot of negative self-talk all the time in my academy. All of my students young and old get caught in society's negative put-down trap, and they don't even know it. It can be very subtle and yet so powerful. The messages we get from the media today are filled with anger, controversy, violence, depression, sex, and quick fixes with mind- and body-altering drugs. It seems like this is the way life is, so people act and react accordingly. They are easily programmed into a counterfeit lifestyle that has no real value. It becomes self-defeating again and again, and they accept the idea that— **Good Enough to Get By Is Good Enough.**

"This is not true," Cliff reiterated. "Unless people develop a desire for excellence and the will to extend themselves in the process, they will not get out of the jungle of life or be able to reach the joy of becoming their best selves.

"Let me share a fitting story that illustrates this:

> A father had three sons who all worked as buyers for the same man, the president of a large import firm specializing in fine items from the Orient. One day the father, who was an old boyhood friend of the president, went down to talk with him. He went into the office and said,

"Jim, my sons all work for you, and I appreciate your company hiring them. I have one question that is bothering me. You pay one of them $400 a week, one them $500 a week, and one of them $1,000 a week. Why?"

The president leaned back in his chair and was silent for a few moments. Then his face brightened as he answered, "Well, maybe I can show you why. Have you got enough time to stay a while?"

"Sure, I can stay all day," the father said.

"Fine, then make yourself at home here in the office, and listen to my conversations with each of your sons."

He picked up the phone and called one of the sons, the $400 son. The president said, "I understand the cargo ship Ontario has just docked at the wharf loaded with goods. Please go down there and see what cargo it is carrying that we might be interested in buying, and let me know." About five minutes later the president's telephone rang, and the young man said, "I didn't even have to go down there to get the information. I just telephoned, and they said they have five hundred bolts of silk onboard." The president thanked him and shared this information with the father.

He then buzzed the next son, the $500 son, and said, "The Ontario has just docked. Will you please go down and see what it has onboard that we might be interested in, and let me know at your earliest convenience?" About an hour later the telephone rang, and the second son said, "I just went down and checked the Ontario. It has five hundred bolts of silk onboard." The president thanked him and shared the information with the father.

He then rang the third son, the $1,000 son, and said, "The Ontario has docked." He told him the same story he had told the other two sons and made the same request. The young man returned four hours later and came to the president's office. "Well, the boat had five hundred bolts of silk onboard, and all are excellent quality. I bought them for $200 each and filled that order we had waiting from one of our customers. He bought all of them from us for $400 each. The Ontario also had 200 oriental rugs. We don't usually handle rugs, but I know who does, so I called him long distance and made the sale. The deal will net us about $40,000. There were also seventy-five jade statues. I examined them and they look beautiful to me, but you are the expert—you always handle the jade trade yourself, so I took an option on them for twenty-four hours so you can have time to go down and look at them and decide."

The president said thanked him, and the young man left. The president then asked the father, "Is the question you asked when you came in answered?"

"Yes," replied the father, "one of my sons didn't even obey you, the other one went only halfway, but the last one gave you everything he had."

"The bottom line of this story is:

LEARN TO TAKE AN ORDINARY JOB AND MAKE SOMETHING OUT OF IT

Gary responded, "That story really illustrates what our best shot is all about. I learned that in my first mountain breakaway with Frosty some years ago."

Cliff continued, "I'm sorry to say that the 'Good Enough to Get By' lifestyle seems to be prevalent among so many young people today. I'm sure Frosty told you about the student, the exam, and the Christmas greeting to the professor."

Gary and Dan nodded and smiled.

"The goal of our martial arts academy is to teach and coach our students on how to become like a third son or daughter. We teach Frosty's four blueprints-for-life attitude games similar to what we are doing this weekend. Everything starts with these. We then develop the martial arts systems that give them a new inner confidence and raise their self-worth.

"To do this we coach our BIG 5: Respect, the Blue Car Attitude, Self-Discipline, Desire and Goal-Setting, and the Rewards of Hard Work. It's exciting to see how people young and old respond as they start to combine their moment-by-moment focus with the physical techniques and systems of karate. We teach this in a friendly, firm, and fun atmosphere that motivates them to give their best shot every time.

"The key to it all is when they discover within themselves how to use their power of choice and start making positive choices in their life through our goal-setting program. Through meaningful repetition they form successful habits that give them confidence and self-worth to take on life's challenges in a positive way. They are then able to handle the constant negative peer group influences in their lives much better.

IT'S NOT THE CRITIC
WHO COUNTS;
IT'S THE ONE IN THE ARENA
WHO GIVES THEIR BEST SHOT
OVER AND OVER AGAIN!

"Martial arts is growing in popularity in our country," Cliff said, "however it is still misunderstood by a large number of people. It is so much more than self-defense techniques and body movements. It is a mental discipline that assists a person to act and react with maximum balance, leverage, and power.

"By learning to maintain a strong focus along with the mastery of karate skills, a person will automatically respond to the events in life in a safe, efficient, and productive manner. This increases their vim, vigor, and vitality.

"There is a classic saying—

IF YOU GIVE A MAN A FISH,
HE EATS FOR A DAY—
IF YOU TEACH HIM TO FISH
HE EATS FOR A LIFETIME

Gary and Dan had both heard this saying before, but it had never meant as much as it did now.

"Believe me, we make fishermen and -women out of *all* our academy students."

Frosty said, "You can see why Cliff's academy has been so successful. It exemplifies the spirit of excellence. It has received numerous awards for outstanding leadership and performance. His program gives people the tools to build a successful life regardless of their present situation."

Dan and Gary wrote another set of notes in their playbook.

Everyone got up and stretched, grabbed some munchies and cold drinks, and sat back down and resumed their conversation.

Chapter 13

Ready—Set—Goals

The key to playing the Challenge Game as well as all the other games in a positive and exciting way is through—

GOAL-SETTING

Frosty looked intently at the guys. "Most goal setting programs, however, are red car models on the **road to success** mentality, where the goal is at the **end of the road**. The day-by-day stuff is just a small part of the action plan. It's all the 'have to' stuff, because with the red model if you don't get to the end of the road, you have failed again. It's the old 'number one or no one' game.

"The constant theme of this model is to work harder and harder. However, when you encounter the many negative situations that will occur along the way, you experience tensions and anxieties...many times followed by fear and regret. These negative emotional feelings undermine confidence and self-worth. In some ways it can become another—**self-fulfilling prophecy**.

"The blue model goal-setting program is a totally different paradigm. The goals here are not at the end of the road—

THE GOALS ARE THE ROAD

"This is a startling difference!" Frosty said. "This model is a powerful force in building confidence and self-worth. We gain new direction and intensity when we make daily and weekly achievement and accomplishment goals in different areas of our lives (physical, mental, social, spiritual, family, financial, professional, and personal).

"These do-it-now targets that we shoot at and hit day after day are invigorating and energizing and confidence builders. We now start to take ordinary things and make something out of them, when before we didn't even see them. The motivational pay value of this is Big Time as we see and feel ourselves closing our potential performance gap in various areas of our life.

"These goals come from the blueprints of our visions and desires. We all need to create dreams and visions in our mind's eye. These are long-range views of where we want to go, what we want to do or become. They need to be planted in our subconscious mind, where we can reflect on them over and over again.

OUR VISIONS ARE
OUT OF SIGHT, BUT NOT OUT OF MIND

and become a self-fulfilling prophecy, for

WE BECOME
WHAT WE THINK ABOUT!

"The key link," Frosty said, " in the motivational chain is **DESIRE**. All achievements, accomplishments, and successes begin with **DESIRE**. It's that fire of **DESIRE** within us that hits our hot button and gets us going. It is what gives us **MEANING AND PURPOSE.**

OUR DESIRES ARE
OUT OF OUR REACH,
BUT NOT OUT OF OUR SIGHT

"**Do-it-now** goals give our desires **direction and intensity**," Frosty said. "They are the high energy fuel that transfers them into momentum in raising our performance level. Working hard is fundamental for all successes, but the real key is to learn how to work SMARTER, not just harder. The acronym SMARTER [1] is in itself an actual system for successful goal-setting:

> S -> SPECIFIC
> M -> MEASURABLE
> A -> ATTAINABLE
> R -> RELEVANT
> T- -> TRACKABLE
> E -> EXTRA EFFORT
> R -> REVISE & RENEW

"When you **ink what you think** and **do it now**, follow this system and get regular feedback that helps you adjust your actions and you will start hitting bull's-eyes right away. It's an exciting confidence builder."

IT'S SO EASY NOT TO DO IT NOW

There is a classic story about how Satan wanted to destroy humanity and rule the world. He called his chief assistants. Anger spoke first "Let me go; I will set brother against brother, sister against sister, man against woman, and woman against man. I will get them all angry at each other and they will destroy themselves."

Next spoke Lust. "I will corrupt human minds. I will make genuine love disappear and turn them into beastly creatures."

Greed stated, "Allow me to go and I will instill in human hearts the most destructive of all passions. Then human's uncontrolled desires will destroy them."

The twins, Gluttony and Drunkenness, stood up and said how they could make human bodies weak and their minds distorted, making them easy victims. Envy, Jealousy, and Hate explained how each of them could destroy humanity. Idleness also claimed he could do the job.

Satan wasn't satisfied with any of these. Finally his last assistant stood up and said, "Let me go and do it. I shall talk to humans about all that God wants each of them to be. I shall tell them how fine these plans are – to be caring, sharing, faithful, and full of hope. To each one I shall talk of the many good purposes of life."

Satan could not believe what he had heard. But his assistant continued, "I shall tell them, however, there is no hurry; they should really do their own thing. They can do all those other things tomorrow. I shall advise them to wait… wait until conditions become more favorable before they start." He then disclosed to Satan that humanity really doesn't know that — the road to hell is paved with good intentions. Satan's eyes lit up. "You are the one – you shall go and destroy humanity." The chosen one's name was Procrastination. He is the one who will convince humanity to put off those Godly things and good intentions a while longer. And as they do, without their knowing it, Satan and his forces will take control of the world.

He was going to be the best he could be –
tomorrow;
No one could be braver or more caring than
he – tomorrow;
A true peak performer is what he will be –
tomorrow;
The story was true when his life was all
through –
He left those things to do – TOMORROW

The bottom line is **DO IT NOW**! For
NOW spelled backwards is **WON**! You will
have WON, when you **DO IT NOW**!

WISHING WELL

Gary responded, "I hadn't thought of
visioning, desires and goal-setting in this way.
My desire is to start to do this for myself, my
family, and my business. I'm sure it will enhance
our trip on our success road."

Frosty smiled. "Here's another story you'll
both like that illustrates this.

Two men applied for a job with a logging
company. The foreman said he had only one
job, but he would give them a fair opportunity

to compete for it. One of the men was a tall, rugged, muscular-looking guy, and the other was short and wiry, with a medium build.

The foreman handed each of them an ax and told them that the first one to cut down ten of the marked trees in the woods ahead would get the job.

The big man laughed to himself as he looked at the smaller man, for he knew he was bigger and stronger. They took the axes, went into the woods, and started chopping down the first tree. After a short time, the smaller man stopped and walked out of the woods. The big man knew he would easily win the job and continued chopping down his ten trees. The little man, however, returned in a short time and started cutting the trees down at a fast pace, in fact, he passed the big man and easily cut down his ten trees first.

The angered and frustrated big man couldn't believe it—how could this happen? How could this little man chop down his ten trees so fast?

As the little man walked by him he shouted out, "How did you do it?" The little man looked him in the eye and replied,

"I SHARPENED MY AX!"

"Working smarter, not harder, is the key," Frosty said. "Working hard is important for success in anything, but we must also learn to work smarter. Let's finish Blueprint for Life #3 with a poem[2] that puts the challenge game in perspective."

As I pause to think of something
That sets us each apart

It seems to me that goals in life
Must be the place to start

Imagine playing football
On an unmarked field of green

No goal line to be sought
No goal post to be seen

It would be an aimless battle
Were there nothing to be gained

Without a thing to strive for
Without a score to be obtained

We must have desires in our life
They're the flame that warms our soul

With our everlasting visions
We can reach them with our goals

Frosty handed out Blueprint for Life #3 for Dan and Gary to put in their playbooks.

BLUE PRINT FOR LIFE # 3
The Challenge Game

ATTITUDE GAMES OF LIFE
LIFESTYLE CHOICES
RED CAR!   BLUE CAR

PROBLEMS ←→ CHALLENGE

(IT'S YOUR CHOICE)

PROBLEMS CAN BECOME A SELF-FULFILLING PROPHECY CAUSING NEGATIVE AND TROUBLED MINDSET OF DOUBTFULNESS, FEAR & FRUSTRATION.

CHALLENGES CAN ENERGIZE US IN A POSITIVE WAY TO APPROACH LIFE'S MANY VARIED SITUATIONS. WE CAN GO FOR THEM WITHOUT FEAR & GIVE OUR BEST SHOT OVER & OVER AGAIN.

2nd EFFORT is the key!

WHETHER WE THINK WE CAN OR THINK WE CAN'T, WE'RE USUALLY RIGHT.	Winston Churchill's Famous 7-word speech.

GOOD ENOUGH TO GET BY IS NOT GOOD ENOUGH.

ACTION ACRONYM TOOL FOR EXCELLENCE

S → SELF TALK → Control negative self talk - it lowers performance

A → AFFIRMATIONS → Positive self talk; Lock on to these to affirm & encourage positive thought patterns → raises performance levels

V → VIZUALIZE → See yourself accomplishing things at a high level → enhances performance

E → EVALUATE → Give yourself regular feedback It's the breakfast of champions. Keeps you on target → RENEW - REVISE & RAISE

LEARN TO TAKE AN ORDINARY JOB & MAKE SOMETHING OF IT. **STORY OF THE 3 SONS**

WHEN WE ARE GIVEN A FISH WE EAT FOR A DAY. WHEN WE LEARN TO FISH WE EAT FOR A LIFETIME.

READY - SET - GOALS

Goal setting & accomplishing them are the key to reaching our VISIONS, DREAMS and DESIRES.

VISIONS and DREAMS are out of sight but not out of mind.
DESIRES are out of reach but not out of sight
GOALS are the DO IT NOWS to reach DESIRES & VISIONS

GOALS ARE NOT THE END OF THE ROAD, THEY ARE THE ROAD.

When we think & feel good about ourselves we produce good results.

S - SPECIFIC
M - MEASURABLE
A - ATTAINABLE
R - RELEVANT
T - TRACKABLE
E - EXTRA EFFORT
R - REVISE + RENEW + REPEAT

INK WHAT YOU THINK

OUT OF ORDER
Wishing Well

PRESSURE & STRESS
There is a BIG Difference

SHARPEN YOUR AXE! [SMARTER, NOT HARDER]
IT'S THE LITTLE THINGS THAT MAKE A BIG DIFFERENCE

.333
[only one]

TOP 10%

out of ten.

.250
lower 50%

A WINNER HAS THE DESIRE FOR EXCELLENCE & THE WILL TO EXTEND HIMSELF IN THE PROCESS OF ATTAINING IT.

DESIRE is the root of all motivation.
THE GREEN FLASH - Yesss!

"It's time for us to go down to the beach to play some beach golf," Frosty said.

Gary and Dan looked at each other and smiled. They were both good golfers and knew this would be fun.

Just outside the door by the steps going down to the beach was a small utility shed. Frosty opened it and got out four nine-iron golf clubs, four different colored golf balls, and three medium-sized bright orange cones. As they went down the stairs to the beach, they saw that the tide was going out and the beach was now over eighty yards wide. Frosty put one cone approximately twenty yards from the steps. Cliff took another cone and angled it some eighty yards toward the ocean, and then Frosty had Gary walk straight down the beach some eighty yards and place the third cone. The three cones were in a triangle.

"Here's how the game is played," Frosty said. We'll divide into teams and our total shots added together for the three holes—hitting the cone—will be the team score. You can smooth out the sand to set your ball down for each stroke. We'll alternate shots. Dan and I will be one team, and Cliff and Gary will be the other. Dan will lead off for our team, and Gary will hit first for yours."

Dan smoothed out the sand for his first shot at the cone—the one near the ocean. He lined it up, took his stance, a practice swing, and then hit a great shot high and long, landing about five feet from the cone. Everyone gave him a big ATTAWAY! Gary's shot was also good, landing about ten feet from the cone—another ATTAWAY! Frosty's shot was short and offline, landing thirty feet from the cone, and Cliff hit a line drive that landed some twenty-five feet to the left of the cone.

Dan lined up for his second shot and hit the cone for a two. Gary took two shots more to hit the cone for a three, and Cliff and I took three more shots for fours.

Dan was getting ready to take his first shot at the second cone across the beach. As he lined up his shot, Cliff asked him, "Dan, do you inhale on your backswing?"

"I don't know I haven't thought about it." He paused for a moment and then took his swing at the ball and abruptly sliced it sharply to the right, the ball going only about forty yards. He immediately pounded the sand with his club and cursed. He looked back at us awkwardly, seeming embarrassed about his negative reaction.

"Cliff has just played a little psych game with you," Frosty said. "It's the distraction game, which if you let it, will get you off balance and keep you from giving your best shot. You lost your center and focus without realizing it and just whacked the ball. Distraction is a simple psych game that we must learn to lock out. A key to overcoming distractions is with positive self-talk. There are actually four basic psych games that prevent you from making your best shot—if you let them get to you. We'll go over these after dinner tonight."

We played the last two cones, and Dan locked out distractions, finishing with two strong shots. Gary finished with a great shot, a hole in one, hitting the last cone on his first shot. High fives and attaways were spontaneous. Cliff and Frosty finished with a three and a four.

Frosty motioned for the guys to come together and sit down on the sand. "This modified beach golf game was just another opportunity to compete to continue learning how to give our best shot by centering and focusing ourselves and locking out all the outside stuff.

"This leads us to our understanding of the differences between stress and pressure. Stress is predominantly a negative emotion that inhibits our performance levels. This happens because of inadequate or nonspecific preparation and/or by getting emotionally out of focus by the mental psych games. This can happen to us quite easily if we don't have the inner games tools to counter them.

"Pressure, on the other hand, can be a powerful positive experience that can bring out high-level performances and accomplishments. People who understand this are able to focus on their specific preparation and transfer it to the pressure situation—this is what clutch players do. They have learned to focus on the NOW—the present action. It's not easy to do, for our mind has a tendency to wander, and we must train ourselves to stay focused and yet relaxed with our total being—our mind, body, and spirit.

"When this becomes a habit, we can see more, hear more, feel more, and do more. We can be quick but not in a hurry. This allows us to look forward to the challenging competitive experiences and compete with a small potential performance gap. It's not size and strength and speed; it's head and heart that really make a difference!

"Here's a great example of the difference between stress and pressure with two baseball players in the same situation."

In a professional baseball game, the home team was trailing 4–3 and up to bat in the last of the ninth inning. There were two out with the bases loaded. The manager put in a young, highly acclaimed rookie as a pinch hitter, giving him the opportunity to win the game. On the first pitch he swung and missed badly on a curveball. On the second pitch he swung late on a high inside fastball. Both pitches were out of the strike zone. The manager, who was a veteran player himself, called timeout and took the bat from the rookie, who was confused, out of focus, and stressed.

The manager put himself in as the new pinch hitter, stepping in the batters' box with no balls and a two strike count on him. He hit the next pitch into right center field, scoring two runs to win the game. The manger was centered, focused, and confident and was at his best in this pressure situation.

Dan shook his head. "I never realized there was such a difference between stress and pressure. I thought they were different degrees of the same thing. It helps to understand that stress is basically negative and that I can eliminate it through specific preparation and the use the inner games tools. I can use pressure to my advantage when I'm prepared and eager to give my best shot in the competitive experience regardless of the odds.

"The beach golf game this afternoon was really good for me. I am trying to understand about locking onto the right stuff we've been learning and not getting caught in the psych game traps and stress situations like the rookie baseball player."

Frosty said, "Dan, figuratively we all strike out, ground, and fly out every day, but we also get our hits too. Here's a good one to think about in baseball. The best hitters go out twice for every hit they get—they are in the top 10 percent with a .333 batting average. The key for them is continuing to give their best shot over and over again.

"A .250 hitter is considered very average, getting one hit out of every four times at bat. The only difference between him and the .333 hitter is one hit out of every ten times at bat. In many ways there is such a small difference between excellence and average."

Dan looked amazed. "It's hard to believe there is such a small difference between them."

"That's why there are so many .250 hitters. They don't understand that small difference, and as a result they just continue hitting at that .250 average."

They put the golf gear by the stairs and jogged down to the beach by Gridiron rock, waded out in the water, and found more colorful rocks for their collection.

They guys had become so absorbed in rock finding that they forgot about seeing the sunset. Realizing that they couldn't get back to the cottage in time, they jogged away from the big rock to get a clear view of the sunset. The sky on the horizon was now very clear with only a few scattered clouds above it. It appeared that they might have a possibility of seeing the green flash!

"The sun moves very fast when it starts to go down beyond the horizon," Frosty said. "Remember, if the green flash happens, it will be when the last part of the sun goes out of sight. Let's start counting down from ten when the sun start to disappear from view."

They waited for a few moments. They started to count—

10—9—8—7—6—5—4—3—2—1

THERE IT IS! THERE IT IS!

A brilliant green emerald flash appeared as the sun went out of sight. It lasted three to four seconds before the green/orange color dominated the horizon.

"Spectacular!" exclaimed Gary.

"What an awesome sight!" Dan said.

"It's truly a special experience that rarely happens. I've seen it only two other times," Frosty said.

They returned to the cottage and charcoaled a steak dinner, ate out on the deck, and enjoyed the multicolored afterglow for some time. Watching these awesome natural highs from God's handiwork was amazing.

Chapter 14

Blueprint for Life #4: The Caring Game

At twilight, the guys moved inside the cottage and built a fire in the large rock fireplace that was quickly crackling and burning brightly. They settled onto the comfortable sofa and chairs.

"It's been a very special day," Frosty said, "and we now have an inspiring evening ahead of us. Here is an interesting handout on your golf game and another one on the basic psych games I told you about before."

Your ATTITUDE is like hitting a golf ball… only you can control its direction

Give it your best shot!

They looked over them, and Dan smiled as he read over the golf handout. He said, "This is what I'm trying to learn. I know what I want to do, but I am struggling to do it."

THE 4 BASIC PSYCH GAMES[1]

DISTRACTION GAME

The opponent's crowd, the arena, signs, noise, etc.—or simple comments or actions to get you to respond to nonessential things.

The Idea: Tries to *distract you from doing what you do*—
getting your focus on other things that aren't important.

The Bottom Line: Everything and everyone are out to get you! Or more subtly,
"Do you inhale when the ball is snapped?"

INTIMIDATION GAME

Another more aggressive version of the distraction game—opponents yell, wise off, put you down. WE PLAY A TOUGH PHYSICAL GAME—we hit on the echo (look out, we're bigger, stronger, faster! We'll push you around!).

The Idea: *Tries to make you afraid* so you will lose your confidence—
lose your belief.

The Bottom Line: Give up now—
you don't have a chance!

PROVOCATION GAME

Opponents provoke you by either ignoring you (showing no interest in anything you do) or by making personal put-downs to you or your team.
This game tries to make you mad and to get you to prove yourself rather than concentrate on your own game

The Idea: *To make you mad* so you will focus on the wrong things—
or try too hard.

The Bottom Line: I can do it—you can't—what you do doesn't matter.

PRETENTION GAME

Opponent makes excuses or downplays his ability, *pretending* he is not very good. Statements like: we'll show up, you are much better than we are, better records, etc. Also claim injuries—best people aren't playing in the game or are playing at half-speed.

The Idea: *Make you feel overconfident* and lose your focus. Attempts to get you
to look ahead to other opponents.
Tries to make you believe you can chalk this up in the "W" column.

The Bottom Line: Opponent says, "You will beat us—
you don't really have to try."

"Some habits are hard to break," Frosty said. "It's like washing your feet and putting on dirty socks. We start with good intentions, but fall back into previous behavior. However, if we are motivated and really desire to change, then with meaningful goal-setting and positive reinforcement, we can develop the new behavior."

Frosty took out two pictures and handed one to Gary and one to Dan. "Tell me, what do you see?"

Dan immediately replied, "I see the face of an old woman."

Gary shook his head. "I see the face of a young woman."

Frosty waited a few moments. "You're both right, but you're both looking at the same picture."

They laid them side-by-side and saw that the pictures were exactly the same.

Dan exclaimed, "If the pictures are the same, how come we see different faces?"

Frosty said, "Because there are two women's faces in the picture—a young woman and an old woman."

They looked at the pictures again for a short time.

Gary then responded, "I can now see both the faces of the young and old woman."

"I still only see the face of the old woman," Dan said.

"Gary, how were you able to see both faces?" Frosty asked.

"I saw the young woman's face right away, and then I closed my eyes and opened them, and looking at the picture from a bigger perspective I saw the other face of the old woman."

Dan insisted, "I still can't see the face of the young woman."

"There are times we may be looking but not really seeing," Frosty said. "In football, we coach our receivers to look the ball all the way into their hands. They think they are doing this, but for some reason when they are looking at the whole ball, it becomes a blur the last few feet as it comes to them—like going through a fog.

"By coaching them to focus only on the tip of the ball they can see it better and can make a greater percent of their catches.

"Similarly, like we did with our receivers, we need to know what to focus on to see what is right in front of us."

Frosty looked at Dan. "Take your finger and cover the mouth and chin of the old woman."

"Aha!" Dan exclaimed. "Now I see the young woman's face."

"It's interesting how people see things from different points of view."

Gary responded, "Like your football player and the worm in the alcohol."

We all smiled.

"The aha experience is always a surprising one, just like you had in finding the face of the young woman," Frosty said. And I believe we are going to have several aha moments tonight as we learn about the last blueprint.

"As you know, we are in the super information age. It's stuff, more stuff, and lots more stuff. The key is getting the right stuff when we want or need it. To do this we need to be motivated to move into action. It's really our MQ—motivation quotient, what moves you to action—not our IQ (intelligence quotient) that is the key to our actions and accomplishments.

"People are basically motivated in three ways: fear, incentive, and love. Fear and incentive are motivators that can produce quick results but lose their effectiveness over time. They are both extrinsic and motivate from the outside rather than from within. Fear motivation is the old kick in the butt stuff. In other words, if you don't do it, you're going to get kicked in the butt. It's all the 'have to' kind of stuff. In this style you endure the trip and do what you have to do, but in the end it leads to mediocrity, for there is no extra effort. You do what you have to do, and that's it. While fear motivation does produce basic results, the relationship is negative, demeaning, and alienating.

"Incentive motivation is the classic 'carrot on a stick.' We see this a lot today, however certain conditions have to be met in order for it to be effective," Frosty said. "The carrot has to be big enough (money, time off, gifts, etc.), it can't be too far away (length of time), and the person needs to be hungry (for what's being offered). In this style of motivation, we always need to have plenty of different incentive gifts. In other words, when you give people something extra, they will produce. For a certain period of time this reward system will work, but again it has to be in the right situations. Eventually, however, mediocrity will set in when people are doing some of the right things for the wrong rewards. They are responding for the rewards, not for the genuine reason of doing the best job they can. Incentive motivation will produce results however many times the relationship is superficial and impersonal.

"The third type of motivation, and the strongest and most lasting, is the intrinsic motivation of love. Love is a basic need of everyone — a genuine, unselfish love that puts a priority on relationships and develops a healthy, resilient rapport among people.

"We're not talking about the superficial physical "love" that is blatantly displayed in magazines, TV, and movies. In fact, that's not really love at all—it's lust.

"The type of love we're talking about is revealed through caring and sharing, and this brings us to our last

BLUEPRINT FOR LIFE #4
THE CARING GAME

"It is the highest level of joy and fulfillment in our lives. It allows us to rise above our own self-oriented nature as we reach out to encourage, support, and inspire others with our time, talents, and treasures. In doing this we give hope and belief to others. This allows them to do more than they really thought they could. In many ways it's like the strawberry jam. Love motivation produces abundant results and is inspiring and empowering."

Dan said, "I got that one—when you cast your bread upon the waters, it comes back with strawberry jam."

"In other words, it's the double-win—when we inspire others, we in turn are inspired in new ways," Frosty said. "There is, however, another mind-set that is prevalent in our society, much like the red car model of winning that so many people have. It is glamorized and promoted by the multimedia and humanistic self-oriented peer groups.

"It's the ALL ABOUT ME GAME that we've talked about before. It attempts to influence and regulate our lifestyles and value systems.

"We are told we must conform to the times, the fashions, the lifestyle, and the groupies. Popular figures in many fields are used as role models in this 'all about me' lifestyle. It can easily become a selfish, ego-oriented view of life—self-indulgence, self-gratification, self-interest, and self-love are all parts of this.

"This strong accent on the self creates a narrow view of relationships because they are tied to a 'what can you do for me' attitude, rather than a shared friendship.

"It's like being in room of mirrors. This room constantly reflects us back to ourselves, and it can easily develop into a lonely and no-win life situation without us even being aware of it. Being surrounded by MIRROR ROOM people, we find ourselves many times alone in a crowd, for relationships are very superficial. Some peer groups are so into themselves that they fail to understand and meet the genuine needs of life.

The caring game, on the other hand, has a room that is in direct contrast. It is the WINDOW ROOM. The focus is not on the 'I and the ME' but on the 'US and the WE.' It brings about a genuine, sharing, and caring attitude that motivates us to be all we can be. It is in reality, the team concept of life **for the true joy of having is in sharing—being a go-giver not a go-getter.** It's making the time to do this, for when we have that sharing heart we experience a genuine joy and fulfillment like no other."

Gary responded "The football love circle you gave me at our last breakaway was a tremendous communicator about love. I enlarged it and made copies for our family. My wife put them in several key locations in our home and we consistently refer to them. They have really helped us understand and communicate love in new ways.

"I have a different illustration this time also in a football context that conveys the same thoughts, feelings, and actions that the Love Circle did."

I handed Dan and Gary a copy of the Love Gridiron.

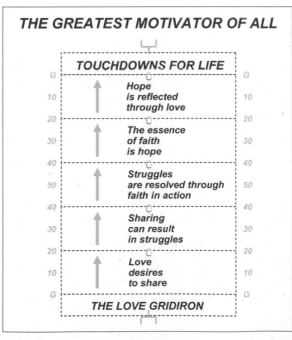

"This is the Blue Car Action Model of the competitive experience in the arena of life. It is a sharing and caring attitude for each other along with mutual respect for others. I'm sorry to say that many Red Car people do not see this as a model of winning and success. They see the Game of Life as well as a football game more like a war game than anything else. They play many of the put-down psych games to attempt to intimidate and belittle others in order to win. The ironic thing, however, is that many times Red Car people focus on the wrong things and end up beating themselves. They never experience the exciting positive enthusiasm in the competitive arena for all they can think about is winning. They lose the value of many relationships and the ability to take ordinary days and make them into good days."

"The Blue Model of the Love Gridiron believes that unselfish love is what bonds a team, a family, a business, or any organization together like nothing else can. It produces special qualities of class and people. These are revealed by their attitudes, actions, and reactions. They don't have to think about them, they just do them."

"This kind of love desires to share and sharing takes many different forms which can bring new levels of fulfillment. Sharing, however, can result in struggles due to our own conflicting desires and mood swings. Many of these come about by the ongoing pressures of society to conform. When our eyes are focused on ourselves, we end up in the mirror room — sharing and the feelings for others lose their significance."

"Many people give up in the struggles of life rather than work through them. We need to learn to be a Tough Minded Optimist, for this is the key for turning struggles into challenges and then, with extended efforts of the right kind, we can overcome them. This is when we find out what the joy of love really is. This is accomplished through FAITH. Our faith in the Lord, faith in ourselves, and those we are with. Faith in action is what brings about new levels of relationships that are built on trust. For there is no tr<u>us</u>t without <u>us</u>. The essence of Faith is hope. Hope is what keeps that fire of desire alive in all of us. This is reflected through unselfish love and it's how we score touchdowns in our lives day after day, week after week, month after month, and year after year."

...FAITH, HOPE, AND LOVE, AND THE GREATEST OF THESE IS LOVE
I CORINTHIANS 13:13

"Much of our inspiration and motivation are found in the Bible," Frosty said. "I John 4:18–19 is real heart power and says it like this: 'There is no fear in love, perfect love casts out all fear, for fear involves punishment therefore the one who fears is not perfected in love and we can love because God first loved us.'

"We can't give away what we don't have, so as we learn to care and share this love in special ways.

"We are a combination of mind, body, and spirit. There is a spirit within each of us that comes from our heart and soul. Many people have hardened their hearts and are in a heart storm much of the time, and they respond to this spirit in highly different ways, beliefs, and lifestyles.

"Just as there are four quarters in a football game, there are four spiritual quarters in life. Everyone is in one of these quarters.

"The first quarter is the atheists. These are humanistic people who have no belief in God and live their lives on their own will and their own power.

"The second quarter is the agnostics. These are the skeptics and doubters about the existence of God. They are free thinking people who, like the atheists, live their lives on their own will and their own power. Both the atheists and agnostics take their life cues from the influences of society they come in contact with.

"The third quarter incorporates many spiritual dimensions. There are all kinds of people that believe in God. Even Satan does—he is God's chief adversary. Many of these gods are very different and are reflected by the various religions of the world. These third-quarter people believe in their god but have no personal relationship with him. They live their lives on their own will and try to gain spiritual power through rituals and works.

"Other third-quarter people are those in the Christian faith who believe in God as revealed through His Son, Jesus Christ. Their faith is based on the teachings of the Holy Bible, and they worship regularly or irregularly in churches, large gatherings, and small groups. Most of them, however, have only a formal or ritual relationship with Jesus. They are still living their lives on their own will, trying to earn Christ's power.

"The fourth-quarter people are Christians who have a deep faith through their personal belief and relationship with Jesus Christ. They have let go of their egos, their pride, and their own power to a power greater than themselves. They experience a peace, power, and joy that passes all understanding. They live their lives on Christ's will and His power.

THIS IS TOTAL RELEASE

"We are all in one of these four quarters," Frosty said. "We have the power to choose which one we are in and this, in turn, affects our beliefs, value systems, and lifestyles.

"There are some uncommon billboards along the highways of our country that catch your eye and challenge your spirit in a very interesting way. Here are a few of them[2]":

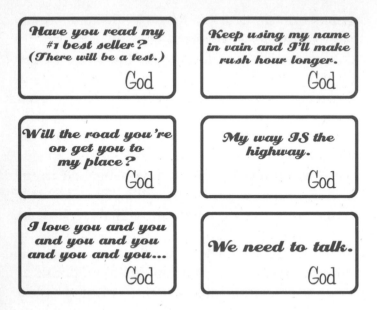

Have you read my
#1 best seller?
(There will be a test.)
God

Keep using my name
in vain and I'll make
rush hour longer.
God

Will the road you're
on get you to
my place?
God

My way IS the
highway.
God

I love you and you
and you and you
and you and you...
God

We need to talk.
God

"Here are a few other zingers."

You think it's
hot here?
God

If you curse,
please use your
own name.
God

"This last billboard reminds me of a classic play that happened in one of our games a few years ago. We had the ball near midfield and ran an end sweep towards our sideline. Our pulling guard threw a perfect body block on our opponent's cornerback and knocked him head-over-heels near the sidelines right in front of me. The cornerback got up in disgust, and said loudly 'Jesus Christ' in a profane way. Our guard got right up with him and said in his face, 'Do you know him?' The opposing player was stunned, not only by the hard block, but by what was said to him. Our guy finished his remark by saying 'I'll tell you about him after the game'."

Gary said, "That was a great response by your player."

"It sure was" replied Frosty. "The other player didn't say anything more."

"For some people, these billboards are like God talking to them. To others, they have no connection at all."

Gary confided, "They do help me to think about my relationship with God."

"The blueprints for life that Cliff and I are sharing with you are from our hearts," Frosty said, "and it's up to you to decide where you are in your life and how you will live it. Let me share a great heartwarming love story with you. It shows how the love and caring from one person to another was able to change their lives and the life of our entire football team, coaching staff, families, and fans.

"It was fifteen years ago in September when this story actually began. During Homecoming week that year our backup quarterback, Paul Finley, was going down the hall of his dorm. One of the rooms was open, and as he went by he noticed a young man in a power-equipped wheelchair.

"He tapped on the partially opened door and walked in. It was here that Paul met Nellie (John Nelson) and where God's magnificent love affair began.

"Nellie was born in Shanghai, China, with arthrogryposis, a rare disease in which none of the joints function below the neck. His body was locked in a fetal position. Nellie was put in an orphanage and not given much of a chance to live. Some Christian mission people were able to get funding to send him to San Francisco, where he was operated on several times to unlock his body. This operation allowed him to be able to sit in a power wheelchair. Years passed, and Nellie ended up at our university on a federal handicap educational grant. He was a sharp, intelligent, young man and had a strong voice, yet he was still totally dependant on others helping him with all his physical needs.

"Nellie had become very depressed with his life. The academic demands to stay in college increased, and he felt he had no purpose or meaning in his life. He had seriously contemplated suicide.

"Paul befriended Nellie that day and invited him to come to our Homecoming football game that next Saturday. He told Nellie he would work out a ride to and from the game and he would talk to me about getting him on the sidelines.

"Nellie was excited and inspired meeting Paul and about going to the homecoming game. He had never been to a football game before.

"On game day, Paul made arrangements to get Nellie to the game. Paul had told me about Nellie, and we got him a pass to be on the sidelines. Our players and coaches welcomed him with enthusiasm and made him feel like part of the team.

"It was an exciting, high-scoring game with the lead changing hands several times. However, our opponent kicked a late field goal to win the game. After the game we have what we call an Afterglow in the field house on our campus where several hundred fans and families gather for fellowship, refreshments, and sharing.

"I usually start the Afterglow program by going over the highlights of the game and other interesting occurrences of the week. Then our captains share and bring up players who played outstanding games. We celebrate birthdays and family/friend anniversaries by singing and giving Attaway cheers. It's a real upbeat occasion regardless of winning or losing the game.

"On this particular day I had an open mic at the end of the Afterglow for anyone who wanted to share. Nellie drove up in his automated chair to the front of the crowd. I held the microphone for him, and everyone quieted down. You could've heard a pin drop. Nellie introduced himself and then boldly told everyone about his life, his depression, and contemplating suicide. He had come to the game and was thrilled to be on the sidelines with the team. When we lost the game, he felt very bad. However being at this Afterglow had changed his life. He thought it would be sad and negative but he said, 'I was all wrong. You may have lost a football game, but you are not losers. In fact, I am inspired not to give up and be a loser myself just because things don't go the way I want. I want you all to know that I'm going to come down to practice each day next week and show you how you have inspired me to be what I can be. To bounce back like you have and renew myself for another week.'

"The crowd stood up and gave Nellie a long standing ovation. Tears streamed down his face as well as the faces of many others. It was a very special time.

"When Nellie came to practice the next week, the first thing we did was present him with two jerseys—one for practice and one for game day, #40. We put the practice jersey on Nellie and told him that he needed to run a forty-yard dash to be an official member of our team. In disbelief his eyes got big and he almost fell out of his wheelchair. We all made a go tunnel for him to drive though in his chair. Everyone was going wild! His time was 16.4 seconds

IT WAS GREAT!

"Nellie has now moved into an assisted living facility near the campus. He comes to the university each day to inspire and have fellowship with the team and student body. Several years ago we made Nellie a member of our coaching staff. He now travels to all of our games and has responsibilities as a staff member. He mentors our younger players, is in charge of recruiting visits, team meetings, and whatever it takes—that's Nellie!

"Several years ago we played in California. Nellie invited the people who had brought him to the United States for his operation when he was young boy to the game.

"He introduced them at the Afterglow. He then thanked them again for caring for him and helping him survive when he was very young. He then said in front of the large crowd, 'While I didn't have any family during the early part of my life, I want you to meet my new family—he nodded toward the crowd. These people love me and taught me how to love. God has given me a plan for my life that has brought me a peace and joy that passes all understanding.' As he finished speaking, the entire Afterglow crowd rose for a standing ovation—many with tears in their eyes. Nellie came to me, looked me in eyes, and said, 'Frosty, I love you—and I responded to him, 'Nellie—I love you.' I gave him a big hug. It was a real heartfelt connection for all of us."

Dan and Gary looked a little choked up at hearing this story.

"Doctors said Nellie wouldn't live much past twenty-five years of age," Frosty continued.

"He is now forty. We had a birthday party for him that over two hundred of our players, families, coaches, and friends attended. It was a memorable night.

"He became active in our Fellowship of Christian Athletes organization on campus and committed his life to the Lord. He has become an inspirational speaker at conferences and events around the country. A documentary film has also been made of his life that has won national awards at both New York and San Francisco film festivals.

"Nellie now has meaning and purpose in his life like at no other time. He is an inspiration to all of us, and just think, it all started when one of our football players befriended him. It shows you how God can use the power of one person to multiply His love a hundredfold.

"That's SOMETHING SPECIAL!"

THERE'S NO ONE ELSE
IN THE WHOLE HUMAN RACE
WITH YOUR KIND OF STYLE
AND YOUR KIND OF GRACE!

Frosty handed them Blueprint for Life #4.

BLUE PRINT FOR LIFE # 4
The Caring Game
ATTITUDE GAMES OF LIFE
LIFESTYLE CHOICES

RED CAR   BLUE CAR

MIRROR ROOM   WINDOW ROOM
it's all about me.   it's all about us.

The 4 Psych Games:
DISTRACTION — INTIMIDATION
PROVOKE — PRETEND
All no-win games — Focus
on the now — what you can
CONTROL!

MOTIVATION
Fear Incentive
or
☆LOVE☆

YOU MAY BE
LOOKING, BUT ARE
YOU SEEING?

TOUCHDOWNS for LIFE
HOPE reflected through love
essence of FAITH is HOPE.
struggles resolved — FAITH in action
Sharing can result in struggle
Love desires to share
THE LOVE GRIDIRON

Total Release

NELLIE
A special kind
of mom →

People don't care how much you know
until they know how much you care.

FAITH, HOPE & LOVE
The greatest of these
is LOVE. 1 COR: 13:13

THERE'S NO ONE ELSE IN THE WHOLE
HUMAN RACE WITH YOUR KIND OF STYLE
AND YOUR KIND OF GRACE.

THE SUCCESS ROAD →
NOT SOMEWHERE YOU GET,
BUT SOMEONE YOU BECOME.

Will the road you're
on get you to
my place?
God

The evening had gone by quickly, and it was close to midnight. As the men got ready to hit the sack, Gary noticed a picture on the wall that resembled the one he had seen in the mountain cabin on his first breakaway. It was a picture of a mountain with a road going up to the top. He looked at it for several minutes and said, "Frosty, the picture I saw at the mountain cabin some years ago fooled me. At first I saw one road, but when I looked at it the next day, to my amazement, I saw two roads. What about this picture?"

"Turn the light switch at the bottom of the picture," Frosty said.

As Gary turned the switch, a light came on revealing another road that led to the top of the mountain. Beside it was a road sign:

THE SUCCESS ROAD
NOT SOMEWHERE YOU GET
BUT SOMEONE YOU BECOME!

Chapter 15

The Starfish

All of us were up early Sunday morning, had breakfast, cleaned and straightened up the cottage, put our luggage in the van, and went down to the beach for the last time.

We sat down on some large driftwood looking out at the big rock and the ever-changing ocean waves. The tide was coming in and the waves were splashing onto the beach near us. There were scattered clouds, the bright morning sun, and a light ocean breeze. It was refreshing and relaxing. All of us were wearing the brown and white shell leis, which we had worn when we started the breakaway together.

Dan commented, "The time has gone so fast, and we have covered so much this weekend. My playbook is filled with diamonds, and as a bonus we saw the awesome green flash."

"These diamonds are for your **diamond mind,** Dan, and believe us their pay-value is priceless," Frosty said.

Gary shared, "It's been another mountaintop—no, I mean top of the ocean—experience. My battery is totally recharged. I am inspired and excited just as I was before! I understand the principle of the empty cup, and believe me I will have an empty cup as much as I can for each life situation, but I do want you and Cliff to know that my cup is running over with the right stuff that you have so humbly shared with us. It reinforces and expands my first BIG TIME breakaway experience with you and has given me an even deeper meaning and purpose in my life and my relationship with God. The green flash was a ten!"

Gary looked at Dan, "I told you we would hear some great stories that would help us to remember key ideas and principles of the blueprints for life."

"That's for sure," Dan said. "I've written the key ideas and principles of the stories in my playbook so I'll remember them and be able to tell them to my wife, family, friends, and associates.

"I was reluctant, skeptical and actually fearful to share my lifestyle when we arrived at the airport. Those feelings soon vanished when we met you two. You both have a way of showing that you care about us before we even got to know each other.

"You gave us four blueprints for life and the tools to build them. You also gave me a new awareness of the power of God's love and my relationship with Him, which I hadn't thought much about. I want to learn more about Him and really try to understand what love is all about.

"You respected me when I didn't agree with you, and you let me work through my struggles in 'unselfing' myself. I still have a long way to go, but I now know that I didn't know—whereas before...

I DIDN'T KNOW
THAT I DIDN'T KNOW!

"This playbook will be my life playbook," Dan said, "and I honestly want to trade in my bright red car thinking for a new blue one. I realize that I will, as Frosty said, 'sometimes—

WASH MY FEET
AND PUT ON DIRTY SOCKS.'

"But I do know that I want to change my attitude toward life, which will affect my thoughts and actions and as a result life's attitude toward me will change.

"You both have been mentors to us this weekend. I respect both of you—who you are and what you stand for. I want to be able to cash those three checks you gave us the first day—having more fun, performing at a higher level, and feeling good about myself and my place in life. I know this won't be easy, for my past mind-set and habits were red car thinking mostly about myself. I know it all starts at home with my wife and family. I am learning what love and caring are really all about, and I want to be able to tell them and show them in genuine humility and unselfishness what this blue car model is all about."

Frosty took a small stick and drew in the sand a square grid like they had in their playbooks. "Here are the basic sixteen squares we started with. You know there are more than sixteen square, as you restructured them. However, looking at it from the outside, it looks the same. It's an inside game—a game of the heart—it all happens inside the lines.

"That is what has happened to you, Dan. You look the same on the outside, but you are a changing person on the inside, and that's where it really counts. Real change has to take place first on the inside to affect our outside actions.

"We've covered so much in a short time and when you go home it will be entirely different. We are in a red car world. You are going to get bombarded with red car thinking and actions. Change can be overwhelming, and it will be so easy to revert back to driving the red car on the road to success. It takes belief, courage, and commitment to build the four blueprints for life—but the pay-value is worth it!! You and Gary need to have regular quality time together to strengthen and affirm each other driving your Blue Cars on the Success Road."

Dan responded, "I know the actions I now want take, and I realize that my thoughts are the key. You have made me realize that

I DO BECOME WHAT I THINK ABOUT!

We all started walking down the beach near the water. Cliff saw a starfish being washed up by the waves. He went over and picked it up and said, "Here is another story about how one person can make a difference."

A young boy from the Midwest had come to the West coast to see the ocean for the first time in his life. It was an awesome experience just seeing the immense size of it. Water as far as you could see. As he was walking down the beach he came upon many starfish that had washed up on the sand. He stopped and started picking them up and throwing them back into the ocean. He kept doing this for a considerable length of time when a lifeguard who was patrolling the beach drove up in his jeep. He stopped, came over, and asked him what he was doing.

The boy replied he was throwing the starfish back into the ocean so they wouldn't die. The lifeguard told him that hundreds of these starfish are washed up on the beach every week. There are so many of them that we scoop them up and put them in garbage cans and haul them away. There's no way to make a difference because there are so many of them.

The young boy looked into the lifeguard's eyes and said, "Maybe I can't make much of a difference with all of the starfish, but I sure can make a difference with this ONE." And he tossed it back into the ocean.

Cliff continued, "You see, it seems like one person can't make a difference—but believe me, we really can if we are willing to make the effort. This poem says it so well.[1]"

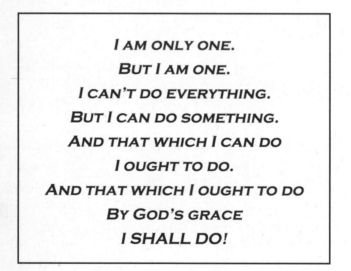

I AM ONLY ONE.

BUT I AM ONE.

I CAN'T DO EVERYTHING.

BUT I CAN DO SOMETHING.

AND THAT WHICH I CAN DO

I OUGHT TO DO.

AND THAT WHICH I OUGHT TO DO

BY GOD'S GRACE

I SHALL DO!

Frosty concluded, "**That's what this weekend has been all about.**"

Chapter 16

The Strange Secret

All of us climbed the stairs by the cottage, got into the van, and started the trip to the airport. Both Gary and Dan were absorbed in their playbooks during the entire trip as Cliff and Frosty chatted with each other.

Approaching the airport, Gary and Dan looked up and couldn't believe we were already there. Frosty stopped at the United unloading zone and let them off to check in while he parked the van in short-term parking.

Frosty and Cliff met Dan and Gary at the security entrance to the concourse. Cliff and Frosty were each carrying royal blue sports bags. Printed on one side were Gary and Dan's names and "Pacific Ocean Breakaway 2005."

"This is a special gift for each of you from Cliff and me," Frosty said. "You are, however, not to open these until your flight is underway and the pilot has turned off the seat belt sign.

Gary, you are to open yours first and follow the instructions, which will tell you and Dan what to do."

Frosty and Cliff bid their friends good-bye with a big hug and a thumbs up. Through teary eyes Dan looked at them, smiled, and turned and went with Gary through the security gates and down the concourse to board their plane.

As the 757 reached its cruising altitude and the pilot turned off the seat belt sign, they put the sports bags on their laps. Gary unzipped his first. He saw a small cassette recorder with a note telling him to turn it on before going any further.

He pushed the play button and the tape began...

"Frosty here. Well, as you know, I'm not actually here, but my voice is here to share with you some final thoughts about our breakaway weekend. First off, Cliff and I want you to know what an inspirational weekend this has been for us—it has meant so much to be with you and to share our four Blueprints for Life and the tools to build them. We have tried to light that fire of desire in your hearts and empower you to take on the challenge of building them.

"You are both special men in your own right—each at a different place in your life. We hope and pray that you will see the pay value of driving the blue car on the success road and experience the true joys of life each day.

"We also were very fortunate to experience the incredible green flash—a rare event indeed, which we hadn't seen in several years. We encourage you to share your weekend and playbook with your wife and family and then in your daily life with your business associates and friends. Believe us, it's our attitude toward life that determines life's attitude towards us, and remember that the goal isn't at the end of the road; the goal IS the road.

"Dan, you should now unzip your bag, and both of you can lower your tray tables. We have five special gifts for you. As you can see, they are numbered on the boxes. Open each one together and talk about the significance it has for you before going onto the next one.

"Make it a good one—we know you will.

"This tape will end five seconds after I finish talking, and your new adventure will begin. Remember…

YOU HAVE THE POWER!

5, 4, 3, 2, 1…
THE CASSETTE SHUT ITSELF OFF

Both Gary and Dan excitedly opened box number one. In it was a bright blue *empty* teacup. They looked at each other and remembered well the story of the grand master and the empty cup. The key meaning of it is that until you empty your mind, like this empty cup, you cannot receive anything. You do this by not being afraid to change and yet not changing for the sake of change. On the side of the cup was the word *GIGO*.

Dan responded, "I remember what that stands for:

> **garbage in—garbage out**
> **good in—good out**
> **God in—God out."**

"What we put in our mind comes out in the form of thoughts, feelings, and actions," Gary said. "It is our choice what we put in it."

They then opened box number two. In it was a model blue car and a plastic road sign marked "The Success Road." They shared with each other the red and blue car models of winning and the two different roads they travel. They acknowledged that they have a choice they didn't realize they had, much like the eagle in the chicken pen.

They now opened box number three, which to their pleasant surprise contained the leather pouch and rocks they had found on the beach. As they started to empty the rocks onto the tray in front of them, they saw that these rocks were different.

They were similar to the rocks they had picked up; only these were brightly colored and polished with double-win thought patterns on them. They picked up one rock of each color and read them.

Written on the white ones were—

"MAKE THE BIG TIME WHERE YOU ARE."

On the blue ones—

"YOU DON'T HAVE A GOOD DAY; YOU MAKE IT A GOOD DAY!"

On the green ones—

"AS IRON SHARPENS IRON, SO WE SHARPEN EACH OTHER."

On the red ones—

> **"IT'S NOT THE CRITIC
> WHO COUNTS;
> IT'S THE MAN IN THE ARENA
> WHO GIVES HIS BEST SHOT
> OVER AND OVER AGAIN."**

On the black ones—

> **"IT'S OUR ATTITUDE TOWARD LIFE
> THAT DETERMINES LIFE'S ATTITUDE
> TOWARD US."**

The orange ones—

> **"IF YOU HAVE CLASS,
> YOU DON'T NEED MUCH ELSE.
> IF YOU DON'T HAVE IT,
> NO MATTER WHAT ELSE YOU HAVE
> IT DOESN'T MAKE MUCH
> DIFFERENCE."**

On the silver ones—

> **"I BECOME
> WHAT I THNK ABOUT!"**

The gold ones—

"CAST YOUR BREAD UPON THE WATER AND IT WILL COME BACK WITH STRAWBERRY JAM."

Gary then explained, "When we apply the double-win thinking of these special rocks to our lives, it gives us another tool to use in building the four Blueprints for Life. We can then motivate our family, friends, and associates by sharing these with them."

Dan responded, "That's for sure—like the silver rock says...

WE BECOME WHAT WE THINK ABOUT

"It is a self-fulfilling prophecy."

They were now ready to open box number four.

Dan remarked, "Frosty told us we would find the Strange Secret of the Big Time, and we haven't found it yet, so it must be in one of the last two gifts."

"He also told us that when we find it we would never be the same."

With great anticipation they opened box number four.

They reached in and took out a small miniature wheelbarrow just like the one Frosty had at the ocean. They remembered the key story of Nick and Jacob on belief and trust.

In each wheelbarrow was a small matchbox. They picked it up, slid the cover open and there was a bright blue card with a message on it in bold white letters.

THE STRANGE SECRET IS THAT THERE IS NO SECRET!

Both Dan and Gary sat stunned for several moments. Gary broke the silence.

He looked into Dan's eyes and said with great emotion, "We knew the secret all the time. That's why there was no secret. We just didn't connect the dots. We talked about it, thought about it, and experienced it this weekend, but we didn't recognize it as a secret. That's why it was strange; it's like the story of the farmer that didn't recognize the acre of diamonds right there in front of him. When we realize that it is a **Power** that can change life from negative to positive, from depression to joy, from mediocrity to excellence, we know what it is."

Dan exclaimed,

IT'S CHOICE— IT IS THE POWER OF CHOICE

It's the last words Frosty said on the tape."

"That's it, Dan. When we focus on the *best* and not the worst, the *beauty* and not the ugly, the *praise* and not the curse, we will reflect these in our lifestyle and will be in harmony in our relationships and our decision-making. Remember when Frosty drew the sixteen squares in the sand our last time on the beach? We knew there were more than sixteen.

"The changes in the total number of squares were inside, the lines just like the power of choice within us."

Gary continued, "Choice is really about our heart, not our head. Our true thoughts and beliefs come from our heart. It is the center and source of our innermost being. When we change to a caring heart, it causes a new way of thinking, which generates faith, hope, and love. We then experience that great life force known as...

HEART POWER
THAT GENERATES
A NEW FULFILLING DIMENSION
IN OUR LIVES!

"I know that's true for that's what happened to me some ten years ago when I experienced my first breakaway," Gary said. "Since that time, I've been able to change problems into challenges in overcoming disappointments and obstacles in my life. The blue car lifestyle on the success road has increased my levels of performance and has helped me feel good about myself and my place in life.

"Dan, when you make the choice to drive the blue car on the success road of life...

YOU WILL, LIKE THE YOUNG EAGLE,
NEVER BE SAME

"For you will:

**MAKE THE BIG TIME
WHERE YOU ARE!**

Gary and Dan sat for some time and thought about the great weekend they had with Frosty and Cliff.

The ocean beach setting had been awesome. They'd had so much genuine fun and had learned a great deal about themselves. They had received an inspiring and informative inner game playbook loaded with an acre of diamonds; they had experienced competition in a new light that changes the game; and they had seen the amazing green flash.

Both men knew they had been part of something very special.

Dan's voice brought them back to the present. "Frosty said there were five gifts, but we've only opened four, and I don't see anymore in the blue bag." They both looked again and found their bags empty.

As they looked through the gifts they had received to see if they had missed it, Gary picked up the blue card with the STRANGE SECRET on it and turned it over. There was a note that said gift number five was in the side zipper pocket of the bag. They unzipped it and took out a multipage scroll with a wide gold ribbon around it.

They untied it, unrolled it, and started to read—--

The Parable of the Rocks

Three men started out on foot across the Makani Desert. It was a two-day trip over deep, loose sand and towering sand dunes that constantly shifted with the course of the wind...

Things went well on the first day as the men traveled a long distance in spite of the intense heat and strong wind. At twilight they reached a small oasis lined with tall palm trees. It was the midpoint of their journey. They were hot and tired, but as they drank the cool water from the deep well and bathed in the small pool, they were revived and refreshed.

As darkness came, the temperature dropped considerably. They gathered some wood and built a fire near the edge of the pool. After eating, they sat by the fire relaxing and talking. Quietly, a tall male figure in a white hooded robe appeared out of the darkness. They didn't see him until he spoke. His low voice was soft, firm, and friendly.

"Good evening," he said. The startled men reached for their rifles, for they feared they were going to be robbed.

The man continued speaking, "Have no fear—I mean you no harm. I have some important instructions for you that will make you **glad and yet sad**."

The three men peered through the darkness to see who this man was. They could see only the long white hooded robe, his piercing eyes, and the outline of his face revealed by the light from the fire.

The man continued, "When you rise in the morning, look across to the far side of the pool, and you will see various colored rocks. Pick up some of each color, put them in a pouch, and tie them to your waist."

The three men looked puzzled but didn't say a word. The man kept speaking...

"Carry these rocks with you until you reach the end of the desert. Do not take them from your waist, and do not look at them until you have completed your journey. If you follow these instructions, you will see me again and you will be

both glad yet sad.

The three men looked at each other, not sure how to react. When they looked up, the tall man was gone. They quickly picked up their rifles and searched the oasis but didn't find a trace of him. Tired and weary, they went to sleep for the night.

At first light, the three men arose. They needed to get an early start, for the roughest part of the journey was ahead. They quickly ate their breakfast and prepared to leave the oasis.

One of the men looked across the pool and was surprised to see many different colored rocks just as the man had described the night before. He called to the other men.

The first man started around the pool to pick up some of the rocks as the man in the white robe had instructed. Another one of the men also decided to go. The third man, however, became impatient and angry with them. He wanted to get started, and there was no way that he would do such a foolish thing as pick up rocks.

The two men gathered up an assortment of different colored rocks, made a pouch out of a piece of towel, and with a thin rope tied them around their waists. As they picked up their personal gear, the third man ridiculed them for doing such a childish thing. He told them that the rocks would bruise their hips and legs and make the hard trip ahead even more strenuous. They ignored his remarks, and the three of them set off across the desert.

The morning quickly became extremely hot, and the wind continuously shifted the sand dunes, making their progress slow and exhausting.

They stopped to rest quite often, huddling together. Each time the third man became more negative and critical toward the other two men carrying the rocks. Their hips and legs, already bruised by the rocks, began to ache, and they still had a considerable distance to go.

Stopping to rest after another long hike through the sand dunes, the third man verbally harassed them again. The second man, who had picked up the rocks, finally had enough of the verbal abuse. He took off his pouch, opened it, and poured out the colored rocks on the sand. The third man laughed sarcastically and said to him, "What did you expect, diamonds?"

The second man felt more foolish than ever. As he kicked the sand over the rocks, he wondered why he had done this ridiculous thing in the first place. The first man still kept his pouch around his waist and said nothing.

The heat intensified as they continued to trudge over the loose and shifting sand. They stopped again to rest. This time both men verbally lashed out at the other man with the rocks.

As they moved on, both men now continuously berated and cursed at him. The man with the rocks felt his hip and leg aching and becoming numb. The rocks seemed to get heavier and heavier. He now thought to himself, While I despise the attitudes and verbal abuse of these two men, they're probably right. Why am I doing this? It seems very foolish indeed. His thoughts continued…about how the tall man in the white robe mysteriously appeared and then disappeared at the oasis was one thing, but more importantly, how he spoke was another. His voice had such authority and yet it was so gentle and compassionate.

His thoughts continued, I believed him, but I didn't know what he meant when he said that I would see him again. Nevertheless, regardless of these other men, I am going to see this **glad, sad adventure through**.

The sun was now setting in the west, and there would only be about two more hours of daylight. The men continued to move on, grumbling and growling at the man with the rocks. Coming to the top of another large sand dune, they looked and saw a small village in the distance. It was the end of the desert, about an hour away. This energized all of them; for they now knew they could complete their journey before dark.

The two men arrived at the outskirts of the village at twilight—exhausted and about ready to drop, yet content that they had completed their desert journey successfully. They came to several large palm trees and a freshwater well, where they stopped, unloaded their backpacks, and drank the cool water.

The man with the rocks had been limping badly and lagged behind over the last mile. When he arrived, both of the other men pointed to his bloody leg and began laughing at him for being so foolish to carry the rocks clear across the desert.

He dropped to his knees, took off his backpack, untied the pouch from his waist, and emptied the contents on the ground.

The other two men were instantly silent—stunned and shocked. To their utter amazement and disbelief, they saw the rocks had turned into precious gems! The white ones were diamonds, the blue ones sapphires, the red ones rubies, the green ones emeralds, the black ones onyx and the multicolored ones opals.

They looked bewildered and couldn't believe what they saw.

The man who carried the rocks looked into their eyes, smiled, and recalled what the tall man in the white robe had told them.

"Follow my instructions and you will be **glad—yet sad.**"

The two men who hadn't heeded his words were mad and sad.

The other man who had was glad, very glad, yet also sad because…he hadn't picked up more rocks!

He looked down again at the precious gems and noticed a rolled-up piece of parchment among them. He picked it up, unrolled it, and saw a picture. He followed the instructions beneath it…

Concentrate fully on the four dots in the middle of this picture for approximately twenty seconds; then close your eyes for ten seconds. If you don't see anything, follow the instructions again, but instead of closing your eyes, look at a light-colored wall or object.

He closed his eyes, and suddenly was amazed to see the face of the man in the white robe.

He truly was the man who gave us one of God's greatest gifts…

The Power of Choice!

Endnotes

CHAPTER 4

1. The "Power of Choice" idea is adapted from "How to Use your greatest power to change your life" by J. Martin Kohe, in: *University of Success* by Og Mandino (New York: Bantam Books, 1982) pp.114-117.

CHAPTER 8

1. The "Potential/Performance Gap" idea is adapted from *Your Attitude is Showing* by Elwood N. Chapman (Chicago, Ill.: Science Research Associates, Inc. 1983) pp. 42-43.

CHAPTER 10

1. "Hocus Focus Cartoon" is used by permission of the Kings Features Syndicate. North America Syndicate Permission. A Unit of the Hearst Corporation (Orlando, FL).
2. Hocus Focus Answers: numbers are switched, home plate is different, position of the football is different, the fence is different, the glove is bigger, and the helmet is bigger on the boy on the left.

CHAPTER 11

1. "Your State of Mind." Ray Eliot *"Proper State of Mind"* audiotape, ca. 1969.
2. "What is Class?" is adapted from *The Edge*, a collection of quotes, poems, and selections edited by Howard E. Ferguson (Cleveland, Ohio: Great Lakes Lithograph Company, 1983) p. 1-1.

CHAPTER 13

1. Based on the SMART acronym found in the book *Leadership and the One Minute Manager®*, by Kenneth Blanchard, Patricia Zigarmi and Drea Zigarmi, (William Morrow and Company, 1985) pp. 89-91.
2. "Goals, Desires and Visions" is adapted from the poem entitled "Goals," written by Art Holst, former NFL official. Ann Arbor, MI.

CHAPTER 14

1. "4 Basic Psych Games" is adapted from *Sports Psyching* by Thomas Tutko, Ph.D. (Los Angeles, Calif.: J.P. Tarcher, Inc. 1976) p.173-179.
2. "God's Billboards" is from *GodSpeaks Devotional* by Cook Communications Ministries. To order, *www.cookministires.com*. All rights reserved. (Tulsa, OK., Honor Books, 2000)

CHAPTER 15

1. "I am only One" is adapted from *Everett Edward Hale Quotes website*. Everett Edward Hale, American author and clergyman.